For Norman Grabo,
whose interest in my work
I greatly appreciate.
            Carla Mulford

JOHN LEACOCK'S

*The First Book
of the American Chronicles
of the Times,
1774–1775*

JOHN LEACOCK'S

The First Book of the American Chronicles of the Times, 1774–1775

EDITED,
WITH INTRODUCTION AND NOTES BY
CARLA MULFORD

NEWARK: University of Delaware Press
LONDON AND TORONTO: Associated University Presses

© 1987 by Associated University Presses, Inc.

Associated University Presses
440 Forsgate Drive
Cranbury, NJ 08512

Associated University Presses
25 Sicilian Avenue
London WC1A 2QH, England

Associated University Presses
2133 Royal Windsor Drive
Unit 1
Mississauga, Ontario
Canada L5J 1K5

The paper used in this publication meets the requirements of the American National Standard for Permanence of Paper for Printed Library Materials Z39.48-1984.

Library of Congress Cataloging-in-Publication Data

Leacock, John.
  John Leacock's The first book of the American chronicles of the times, 1774–1775.

  Bibliography: p.
  Includes index.
  1. United States—Politics and government—Revolution, 1775–1783—Anecdotes, facetiae, satire, etc. 2. Massachusetts—History—Revolution, 1775–1783—Anecdotes, facetiae, satire, etc. 3. Political satire, American—Massachusetts. I. Mulford, Carla, 1955– . II. Title. III. Title: First book of the American chronicles of the times.
  E211.L44 1987   973.2'7'0207   86-40594
  ISBN 0-87413-305-X (alk. paper)

PRINTED IN THE UNITED STATES OF AMERICA

For J. A. Leo Lemay

Contents

Acknowledgments
Introduction   11
The Text: *The First Book of the American Chronicles of
  the Times*   51
Notes to the Text   81
Appendix A: The Satire and the Play   108
Appendix B: List of Characters   110
Appendix C: Selected Documents   113
  1. Thomas Gage's "Proclamation for the Encouragement
     of Piety and Virtue"   113
  2. An Account of the Powder Scare   114
  3. Gage's Proclamation Proroguing the General Court   115
Bibliography   117
Index   123

Acknowledgments

I thank the staffs at the American Philosophical Society, the Historical Society of Pennsylvania, and the New-York Historical Society for their assistance over the past few years with the Leacock family documents and other relevant materials.

My colleagues at the Pennsylvania State University asked the probing questions that resulted in a final revision of the manuscript. I'm grateful for their interest in the satire. I am grateful, too, to Villanova University for having supported my research and writing during the summer 1985, when I worked on this and other projects.

Professor J. A. Leo Lemay suggested this project, sent me to the key advertisement identifying Leacock's authorship, and advised me on early drafts. Professor Lemay's rigorous questioning, his untiring interest, and his expert guidance have been a continual source of intellectual inspiration. I dedicate this volume to him with affection and respect.

Introduction

The First Book of the American Chronicles of the Times, a parodic satire written as a six-chapter pamphlet series, is clearly one of the most humorous works of patriot propaganda to have come out of the events just preceding the Revolutionary War. A conflation of the political events of 1773 and 1774 in a "biblical" narration, the *American Chronicles* targets both New England and old in a sometimes scurrilous attack on tyranny, militarism, Catholicism, Puritan millennialism, and extremes of all forms. Clearly and consistently anti-British, the text celebrates as folk heroes Benjamin Franklin, Israel Putnam, Samuel Cooper (well-liked pastor of the Brattle Street Church in Boston), a fictional Indian chief, and Oliver Cromwell. The double-voicing of the parodic form enables serious implications—by way of satiric correction—to modify the Cromwellian celebration.

The Puritan vision was popularly conceived as an appropriation of the biblical prophecies to justify the millennial zeal for revolution.[1] During the eighteenth century, belief that the millennium was approaching and that the present confusion was a sign of the future peace existed concurrently with deistic belief that the creation of social contracts was necessary because God was absent. Patriot ministers attempted to re-constitute Bible prophecy as American history perhaps less to convince educated listeners of the coming millennium than to indicate the similar ideological positions held by Whig politicians and biblical patriarchs—that tyranny and oppression were insufferable evils.

The re-contextualization of the Bible text in the new parodic text as *American Chronicles* offered readers the possibility of humorous self-recognition (that millennial zeal was not so different from zeal for tyranny) while it celebrated the cause of freedom. The double-voiced message was available precisely because of the form of the text as parodic biblical satire. *The First Book of the American Chronicles of the Times,* immensely popular in its own day, provides readers interested in parodic texts and in American literature, history, and religious philosophy yet another piece of evidence that the American populace during the Revolution was capable of a complexity and a self-humor often unrecognized by the nineteenth-century historians of American literature.

The First Book of the American Chronicles of the Times has proven to be an intriguing puzzle to scholars. Moses Coit Tyler pointed out in 1897 that "this vivacious specimen of American humor," a "remarkable piece of humorous literature," undeservedly "seem[ed] to have fallen almost entirely out of men's notice."[2] The satire was again taken up in 1907 by M. Katherine Jackson, who reported that the *American Chronicles* "rises above the level of the ordinary pamphlet."[3] In 1926 George Everett Hastings, while demonstrating that Francis Hopkinson did not write the pamphlet series, commented that in this "vivacious" pamphlet, "[t]he use of archaic language in narrating contemporary events is skilfully managed so as to produce some very ludicrous effects."[4]

Interested but unsuccessful in locating the author of *The First Book of the American Chronicles of the Times*, J. R. Bowman wrote a piece identifying the many printings of the satire. The editors of the new journal, *American Literature*, thought the results of Bowman's work important enough to publish during the journal's first year. Having found that the American Chronicles "have interest for the student of American literature because of their humor and the historical events related," Bowman "offer[ed] this bibliography in the hope that it may be of some value to a future investigator" for the author of the satire.[5]

Future investigators there were. But none—until now—has been able to identify the author of the propaganda series. Arthur M. Schlesinger, Bruce Granger, and Bernard Bailyn all admired the *American Chronicles*. Schlesinger called the satire the "supreme example of patriot propaganda written in a satirical vein" and added that "to a people steeped in the Bible nothing could have been more titillating."[6] Granger found the *American Chronicles* "the most ambitious and nearly successful of half a dozen Biblical imitations which appeared in the Revolutionary period."[7] Bailyn decided that the propaganda series was "so complete in its plot and characterization as to make identification of people and places an engaging puzzle," and, he asserted, "By its extensiveness and detail, by the sheer number of its imaginative touches, it attains a considerable effect."[8] Scholars today will find in the form of the *American Chronicles* as parodic satire and in the complex parodic use of apocalyptic and millenial traditions, of folk heroes, and of American patriot zeal a sophisticated patriot statement in behalf of moderation.

John Leacock, Author

Scholars have continued to wonder about the identity of the author of *The First Book of the American Chronicles of the Times*. Bowman's search for the author, the most detailed, yielded no evidence. Moses Coit Tyler had suggested Francis Hopkinson as the author, but George Everett Hastings demonstrated that Hopkinson was not a likely candidate for authorship.[9] Bailyn and Granger made no clear attempts to name the author of the satire.

John Leacock (1729–1802) wrote *The First Book of the American Chronicles of the Times*, as evidenced by an advertisement in the New York *Constitutional*

Gazette. Leacock is already known to readers of patriot propaganda as the author of two texts. The first, *A New Song, On the Repeal of the Stamp-Act* (1766), celebrated the repeal of the Stamp Act of 1765 and denounced the British ministry, especially George Grenville, John Huske, and John Stuart, third Earl of Bute.[10] Its folk hero, Great Commoner William Pitt, Lord Chatham, was praised as the "politic Messiah" who beat the Devil's men in the ministry.

The other propaganda piece Leacock is known to have written is the patriot play, *The Fall of British Tyranny* (1776). Clear evidence of Leacock's authorship of the play was not found until the middle of this century, but by the 1850s scholars had nonetheless considered Leacock the author of the play. Attributions have varied. In Watson's 1850 *Annals of Philadelphia*, "J.H.J." from Ohio is said to have reported that "Joseph Lacock, Coroner . . . Wrote a play, with good humour, called 'British Tyranny.'" Drama historians William Dunlap (in 1832) and James Rees (in 1845) erroneously mentioned Leacock as the author of *"Disappointed"* probably *The Disappointment*, perhaps by Thomas Forrest);[11] but neither spoke of Leacock's having written *The Fall of British Tyranny*. From independent research, Joseph Sabin established and recorded positively that John Leacock wrote the play. In 1886, Charles R. Hildeburn wrote that the play was "said to have been written by 'Mr. Laycock of Philadelphia,'" but in 1889, George O. Seilhamer believed the play's author unknown. Thereafter, Paul Leicester Ford, Oscar Wegelin, and Montrose J. Moses all positively attributed *The Fall of British Tyranny* to John Leacock.[12]

By 1954 Francis James Dallett, Jr., had accumulated enough biographical evidence about Leacock to conclude the play was his. And evidence from Leacock's commonplace book (located at the American Philosophical Society), including records of play pamphlet sales and receipts, indicates that Leacock wrote the play.[13] The commonplace book reports, for instance, in an entry dated 20 July 1781, that Leacock "Left with Mr. Walter to Sell 24 dozens of Plays at 8 dollars per Piece. . . . Left with Mr. Barnard some plays to Sell 12 dozen." Although Norman Philbrick in his introduction to the play in the anthology *Trumpets Sounding* does not attribute the play to Leacock, Leacock clearly wrote *The Fall of British Tyranny*.[14]

Leacock's authorship of the play provides the link to his authorship of the parodic satire. An advertisement for *The Fall of British Tyranny* in the New York *Constitutional Gazette*, 3 July 1776, announced the printing of the play, "Just arrived from Philadelphia," and used as a selling point that it was "By the Author of the American Chronicles of the Times." This key advertisement establishes that John Leacock, the author of *The Fall of British Tyranny*, wrote *The First Book of the American Chronicles of the Times* as well.[15]

Internal evidence from the two works seems to support this conclusion. *The Fall of British Tyranny* contains a direct reference to the *American Chronicles*. In the play, when Lord Boston (Thomas Gage) announces to his associates that the

British "must act on the defensive this winter," Admiral Tombstone (Thomas Graves) bursts out: "Defensive? aye, aye—if we can defend our bellies from hunger, and prevent a mutiny and civil war among the small guts there this winter, we shall make a glorious campaign of it indeed—it will read well in the American Chronicles."[16] Other elements indicate common authorship for the two patriot pieces.

Both the play and the parodic satire use some of the same fictional devices; both use or mention some of the same Bible personages; and both echo some of the same biblical passages. Appendix A discusses the similar fictional devices, biblical personages, and biblical passages found in the play and the satire.[17]

The Fall of British Tyranny and *The First Book of the American Chronicles of the Times* reveal Leacock to have been a well-read man who knew the appeal of Whig principles couched in biblical analogy to encourage colonial patriotism. The play is a more generalized plea for resistance; the satire, a plea particularized for a Philadelphia audience. Indeed, it was this Philadelphia viewpoint, perhaps, that caused Tyler to attribute the *American Chronicles* to Francis Hopkinson. But the satire was written by Philadelphian John Leacock.

Born on 21 December 1729, Leacock was one of a family prominent in Philadelphia.[18] His father, John Leacock (1689–1752), was a prosperous pewtersmith and shopkeeper who had come to Philadelphia from Barbados to invest in land and in the earliest iron furnaces in the province. This John Leacock married Mary Cash (1694–1765) in 1715 in Christ Church, where he served as a vestryman. Of ten children born to the Leacock couple, five reached adulthood.

Little is known of their son John Leacock's early years. Like his two brothers, he was probably apprenticed while young to an established gold- and silversmith. By the early 1750s the younger John Leacock owned his own business in the trade. Having married Hannah McCally in August 1752, Leacock began a family. When his father died late in that year, he gained an inheritance that enabled him to move the smithing trade from Walnut Street to a location (as advertised in the *Pennsylvania Gazette*, 29 November 1753) "opposite Mr. Norris's Alley, at the sign of the Golden Cup" on Front Street, the center of Philadelphia gold- and silver-smithing.

One of Leacock's works in sterling, probably datable to the mid-1750s, is a lovely bauble—an ornately scrolled whistle, decorated with several bells, with a teething stick fitted into the end—now owned by the Philadelphia Museum of Art. Its chased scrolls and flowers are evidently characteristic of mid-century Philadelphia design, but such chasing is considered rare in the Philadelphia silver trade. The whistle, which carries the inscription "S. Morris" and the (scratched in) date "1760" was probably made specially for a child of Captain Samuel Morris.[19] Leacock's trade seems to have brought him the patronage of families wishing to own special pieces not found on the general market. His craft seems to have brought in elements of the engraver's and printer's trades as well, as indicated by several entries on engraving and metalworking in his commonplace book. His will indicates that Leacock left to his son Samuel a copper plate engraving of characters based on the same theme as *The Fall of British Tyranny*.

Leacock's interests in a variety of scientific and cultural concerns complemented those of other family members—printer brother-in-law, David Hall; lawyer brother-in-law, James Read; and cousin-in-law, Dr. Benjamin Franklin. (Leacock and Franklin's wife, Deborah Read, were second cousins.) In the 1750s and 1760s, Leacock entered the social and political scene. He signed the petition to the Proprietors for grounds for St. Peter's Church (1754), and in 1759 he became a member of the State in Schuylkill Fishing Company, which included Philadelphia's most prominent citizens. In addition to writing *A New Song, On the Repeal of the Stamp-Act* (1766), Leacock joined other well-known Philadelphians in the Stamp Act protest by signing the Non-Importation Agreement of 1765. Leacock's signature is significant, for as a tradesman and merchant, he stood to lose business with the ban on importation.[20] By the late 1760s, Leacock had evidently gained such prominence that he could retire to the country to take up the pursuits of a farmer. He left his business in the city in the fall of 1767 and bought an estate in Lower Merion, about seven miles west of Philadelphia. In December 1767, Hannah McCally Leacock (his wife of fifteen years) died, and John Leacock began to devote an increasing amount of time to public projects.

Through the American Philosophical Society Leacock sought the promotion of a public vineyard.[21] Having traveled to Madeira between 1769 and 1771, Leacock became a wine and grape importer.[22] In 1772, Leacock spoke to some members of the Society who encouraged his proposal to develop a public vineyard; he asked Thomas Coombe to present to the Society a formal proposal on the promotion of local vine culture through the use of a lottery.[23] Evidently unsuccessful in the endeavor, Leacock perhaps continued his efforts to convince the public about the prospect of growing grapes by writing articles on vine culture for the *Pennsylvania Gazette*.[24] Leacock married Martha Ogilby in June 1770.

In May 1772, he joined the Philadelphia Sons of Liberty in the formation of a new group, the Society of the Sons of Saint Tammany, named to commemorate an early chief of the Delawares. Both the Sons of Liberty and the Sons of Saint Tammany promoted the patriot cause. Leacock's Stamp Act song, his play *The Fall of British Tyranny*, and his parodic satire all evidence his concern to propagandize for the masses the patriot position. In 1779, Leacock was in Easton and Reading, signing bills of credit of the United States; in 1780, he moved back to Philadelphia and gained the post of Philadelphia coroner in 1785. Leacock evidently spent much of his life in social, political, and literary prominence. He died 16 November 1802, and was buried in Christ Church cemetery in the corner near his relative, Benjamin Franklin.

The Boston Tea Party, the Initial Event

In passing the Revenue Act of 1764, Parliament gave Britain the right to create import duties—not to regulate trade but to gain revenues. Americans questioned Parliament's right to control taxation while preventing the appointment of colonial representatives to Parliament.[25] The Stamp Act of 1765 so angered patriots that they forced the resignations of stamp agents and enacted their own nonimportation measures; the Stamp Act was repealed a year later. By 1767, American concern about taxation without representation was again tested with the imposition of the Townshend Acts, which brought on mob violence and increased nonimportation in the colonies. Parliament repealed the Townshend duties in 1770—except for the duty on tea.

Many colonists boycotted tea, for they believed the partial repeal an insult. Politicians insisted that drinking tea was unpatriotic; doctors, that it was unhealthful. Merchants began to smuggle Dutch tea past British authorities. The smuggling combined with the boycott of British tea to bring about the demise of the British East India Tea Company. By enacting the Tea Act of 1773, Parliament attempted to aid the near-bankrupt company by allowing the East India Company to bypass the merchant middlemen and sell tea directly to colonial consumers.

Colonists feared that the elimination of tea merchants would spread to other imports and cripple the growing trade economy. They viewed the Tea Act as even more inimical than the Townshend duties, so they intensified the boycott. When ships bringing the first consignments of tea arrived in late 1773, the colonists greeted them with urgent pleas that the ships sail home. Finally, after several ships had turned around, Massachusetts Governor Thomas Hutchinson refused to permit any ship to leave Boston harbor without first unloading its cargo. In response, the people of Boston and surrounding communities boarded the ships and dumped tea into the harbor on the night of 16 December 1773. The first chapter of *The First Book of the American Chronicles of the Times* begins with allusions to this event.

The opening verses indicate that the setting for the *American Chronicles* is in London, the city "afar off." The events that occurred immediately after the Boston tea party are detailed, as Mordecai (Benjamin Franklin) shows Rehoboam (George III) and the Sanhedrim (Privy Council) the letters in which Judas the Parasite (Thomas Hutchinson) misrepresented the political and economic situation in Boston. Mordecai is denounced on the floor of the House of Commons by the Wedderburnite (Alexander Wedderburn), and Mordecai loses his postmaster-generalship. A number of pernicious acts (the Intolerable or Coercive Acts) are imposed on Boston, and the King asks Thomas the Gageite

(Thomas Gage) to take over military concerns there. After the first few verses setting up the argument of the parodic satire, the setting shifts to Boston.

The reaction in Boston is led by the activities of the central character, Jedediah the priest (probably Samuel Cooper of the Brattle Street Church), and his allies, Jeremiah (probably Charles Chauncy), Obadiah (probably John Hancock), and Aminadab (probably William Cooper).[26] But other characters appear as well. The three most noteworthy are the Indian chief Occunneocogeecococacheecacheecadungo (Leacock plays on the cult of the Indian, particularly on admiration for Indian war prowess); Phineas (Israel Putnam, legendary hero from the French and Indian Wars, particularly the Battle of Louisburg); and Oliver Cromwell (the great Puritan hero).

While the Massachusetts delegates are meeting at the House of the Carpenters in Philadelphia, the people of Boston decide they need advice. So Jedediah, Obadiah, and Aminadab go to the local witch, Mother (or Sister) Carey, Obadiah's favorite charmer. In a wonderful section of the satire replete with sexual punning and double entendre, the three men convince Mother Carey to use her charms to raise up Oliver Cromwell from the dead. Asking Jedediah to keep it a secret, Mother Carey satisfies their desires and raises Cromwell. Cromwell, after being praised for his prowess, tells the men he will help the colonists and asks them to call Occunneocogeecococacheecacheecadungo and Phineas to arms. He then disappears. And the star Venus becomes dull and drowsy, and the three men depart from Mother Carey.

Cromwell the next day appears in a dream to Gage, who wakes up trembling and faints when he learns of the luminations in Boston that celebrated the Massachusetts delegates' return from the First Continental Congress. Jedediah the priest reads a proclamation from Cromwell. And Simon, Gage's inebriated chaplain, convinces Gage that Cromwell's appearance was not imaginary but real. The sixth chapter, the last to have been printed, consists of parodic versions of the warnings that the First Continental Congress sent to Gage and to the king. The usual "To be continued" notice appears at the end of the sixth chapter, but this chapter seems to have been the conclusion of the pamphlet series.[27]

The events that comprise the basis of the parodic narrative took place between December 1773 and the late fall of 1774. The text does not narrate the events in strict chronological sequence. Nor does it offer its narration by adapting the events of a sequentially devised biblical imitation. That is, parts of a verse in the *American Chronicles* might be adapted to the language of a verse from I Chronicles, juxtaposed with Matthew, or Daniel, or some other biblical book. Very few consecutive verses in the parodic text are sequential appropriations of biblical texts. The disparity of both the chronological events and the biblical texts, the disjunction of the expected time and text sequences, adds to the humor and the complexity of *The First Book of the American Chronicles of the Times*.

The Characters

Bernard Bailyn's comment that the *The First Book of the American Chronicles of the Times* "is so complete in its plot and characterization as to make identification of people and places an engaging puzzle"[28] is an understatement about the attempt to connect the fiction with the fact. Of course, characters such as Monsieur de la Cutta de Bearda (Thomas the Gageite's barber), Simon (Gage's chaplain), and the Indian chief Occunneocogeecococacheecacheecadungo appear primarily for their humor. But even these characters, like Cromwell and Phineas (Israel Putnam), imply the patriot propagandist message. The barber and chaplain both, for instance, are portrayed in such as way as to represent the colonists' anti-Catholic bias (i.e., the barber is French; the chaplain, Catholic). The anti-Catholicism rests on the author's expectations about the Puritan assumptions—held in England as much as in the colonies—that Protestant countries enabled freedom to flourish while Catholic kingdoms insisted upon its demise.[29]

Cromwell, the Indian chief, and Phineas all assert their might as right. Patriot propagandists played upon the colonists' popular views that they were inheritors of the Puritan character and strength of their ancestors. Threatened by the British attempt to impose hierarchy both civil and religious, the patriots asserted that their rights as free Englishmen, rights made available in the colonial charters, were being usurped. That Occunneocogeecococacheecacheecadungo is characterized as willing to fight for the colonists implies at least two ideological statements: the indirect assertion that the colonists were seeking only their natural rights, and the direct assertion that they were likely to win in the battle because the Indians would join them in the fight. The Indian art of warfare and Indian heroism had come to be greatly admired in the colonies.[30] Thus, even those characters that provide incidental humor also enable the propagandist to stress patriot ideology. But note again that the nearly tyrannic zeal with which the patriot position is asserted is also part of the message of this parodic satire. The section below on the significance of the *American Chronicles* discusses more fully the implied message of the satire.

The "biblical" narration invites speculation as to the contemporary identities of most characters. Many characters have biblical names. The question arises, then, as to whether the contemporary personality resembles its biblical namesake. That is, is the name Jeremiah, for instance, given to a person who was like a "jeremiah" to the people of Boston? More than simply an "engaging puzzle," the *American Chronicles* includes characters that, when identified with their contemporary figures, could provide valuable insight into the popular conceptions of contemporary revolutionary leaders. Appendix B is an alphabetical list and index of the characters appearing or mentioned in the *The First Book of the American Chronicles of the Times*.

* * *

Several characters' identities are obvious because all or part of the names of their historical counterparts appear in the text. About half of these are British or British sympathizers. Mansfield, Bernard, Hutchinson, Louis the King of France, Pope Gregory Hildebrand, and Carolus the King of Spain are simply named. Allusions are made also to the Bernardites and Hutchinsonians. In addition, the person called the Wedderburnite is a clear reference to Alexander Wedderburn; Thomas the Gageite is Thomas Gage; and Johnny the Buteite refers to John Stuart, third Earl of Bute. Finally, the Tory propagandists, the Coo-r-ites, and their "letter presser," R----g--n, are obvious allusions to Miles Cooper and James Rivington.[31]

The characters identifiable by name and used in patriot defense largely have to do with Cromwell and his "tribe of Oliverians" catalogued in his "proclamation." Allusions to the Pittites (followers of William Pitt, of course) occur, and the "immortal" Wolfe is invoked. The colonial audience certainly knew the person identified as Matherius Cottonius, and those who read the papers knew of the Maryland tea consignees, Joseph, James, and Anthony. The Massachusetts delegates are easy to identify: Thomas the Cushingite, the Adamites, and Robert the Painite. Of those characters identifiable because all or part of their names appear, only two have principal parts in the satire—the two powerful adversaries, Thomas the Gageite and Cromwell.

* * *

A majority of the characters in *The First Book of the American Chronicles of the Times* are given biblical names. Some of these are easily connected with the contemporary people they represent. Rehoboam is obviously King George III; his adversary in Privy Council, Mordecai the Benjamite, clearly Benjamin Franklin. Haman the Northite is Lord North. And Balaam the wizard, who was ousted by Matherius Cottonius, is Sir Edmund Andros. Finally, Judas the Parasite is Thomas Hutchinson.

The identities of other characters given biblical names in the satire are not so easily established. Perhaps known to contemporary readers, their identities have been obscured by time, if they indeed were ever completely known by the uninitiated popular reader. At least three historians have been intrigued enough by the *American Chronicles* to have attempted identification of characters. All three have been anxious to have Samuel Adams play a part. Moses Coit Tyler identified Jeremiah as Samuel Adams, as did Arthur Schlesinger.[32] Bruce I. Granger believed Adams was Jedediah, perhaps because Jedediah figures so largely in the *American Chronicles*.[33]

In fact, it is more likely that Leacock is depicting religious rather than civil leaders as central characters in the text. If only because the form of the *American*

Chronicles is parodic biblical satire, the personification of religious leaders would be suitable. But also, with the depiction of religious leaders in Boston, the parodist can more readily separate Gage, the secular "Captain of the heathen" from the Boston leaders of the righteous, God's "chosen people." Finally, the major events in the satire that detail Jedediah's and others' activities in Boston occur while the First Continental Congress is convening in Philadelphia. This would mean that Samuel and John Adams, Thomas Cushing, and Robert Treat Paine are not likely candidates as fictional actors, for according to the fictional world of the parodic satire, these men are in Philadelphia, not Boston. It seems, then, that Jedediah and Jeremiah do not represent Adams or secular leaders. Both probably represent two of Boston's leading religious figures.

• • •

Called a scribe at one point (1.18) but called a priest thereafter, Jedediah is one of the more intriguing characters of *The First Book of the American Chronicles of the Times*. That the name Jedediah is used first for a scribe and then for a priest perhaps indicates two men of the same given name. The two men having the same given name and prominent in civil and in religious affairs prior to the Revolution were, respectively, Samuel Adams and the Reverend Dr. Samuel Cooper. According to Clifford K. Shipton, "Sam Cooper and Sam Adams . . . were the nucleus of an underground which waged unceasing war against the Crown's representatives in America."[34] Mentioned only once, Jedediah the scribe (probably Samuel Adams) is the less important of the two Jedediahs in *The First Book of the American Chronicles of the Times*. If the name Jedediah refers to only one person, then that person is Samuel Cooper.

Jedediah the priest is the central patriot character in *The First Book of the American Chronicles of the Times*. Not only does he have "understanding of the times to know what the Americanites ought to do, and what they ought not to do," but "all his brethren were at his commandment" (1.21). Worried about the "evil that has been brought upon our . . . New Canaan" (1.36), Jedediah the priest continually checks to see that the patriot action "proceedeth of the Lord our GOD" (1.38), and he explains the patriot position in biblical terms. He is as attractive to Mother Carey (chap. 3) as he is to his congregation. When he reads the congressional report to his congregation, "all the people . . . listened unto him with great attention, for the words of his mouth were sweeter than honey, and the sound of his voice like unto a trumpet, which reached from one end of the land to the other" (6. paragraph 49). Jedediah's personal appeal, his interest in political affairs, and his use of biblical texts to explain the patriot situation all point to Samuel Cooper.

The Reverend Dr. Samuel Cooper, one of Boston's distinguished Congregational ministers, pastor of the Brattle Street Church, was viewed by the foremost of Massachusetts loyalists as one among Boston's most influential politicians.[35] Cooper was grouped with Samuel and John Adams and John Hancock as a principal leader of the resistance to Britain. Although the clergy was generally reticent about espousing patriot resistance, Cooper clearly favored the patriot cause and regularly met with radical leaders.[36] Cooper understood well the social, economic, and political implications of resistance to the Crown. Franklin, in fact, made Samuel Cooper his chief confidant in New England.[37] Hutchinson evidently feared the Saturday meetings of "Otis and the two Adams, Cooper and Church."[38] He disliked, too, the power of the Boston clergyman, probably Cooper, "who has such influence in our political measures."[39] Well Hutchinson might have feared Cooper, who preached to Boston's elite in the Brattle Street Church and who used the Brattle Street parsonage for meetings with Otis, Hancock, and Samuel Adams. In fact, early historians held that the famous "Hutchinson" or "Whately" letters that Franklin somehow acquired and mailed to New England had been addressed to his good friend, Samuel Cooper.[40] Cooper was credited by his contemporaries with many of the political essays that appeared in the *Boston Gazette* and *Independent Ledger*.[41] His letters to Franklin from the period 1772–74 reveal his thorough knowledge of patriot affairs.[42]

Especially important to the patriot cause was Cooper's influence over his parishioners. Sprague's *Annals* records a statement by an anonymous young contemporary who believed Cooper's preaching

> was well nigh unrivalled in the pulpit during the period in which he lived. With a fine commanding person, and a voice of great sweetness and power, he united a remarkable fluency of utterance, as well as grace and force of expression, and appropriateness and energy of thought, which never failed to arrest and hold the attention of his audience.[43]

Jonathan Belcher's is a more constrained but equally commendatory account:

> I got Mr. Cooper, to preach, both parts of the Sabbath, to a pretty numerous auditory, for that place, on which Occasion, I enjoyed more Satisfaction, than I can easily express. He is a Sweet, and most exi[ ] preacher, a great Honour to his late Fathers Memory and to himself.[44]

Cooper, an attractive and persuasive minister, evidently pleased his listeners in manner and matter both.

Indeed, Cooper's persuasiveness, along with that of most other Boston clergy, probably came from the sometimes vague, sometimes rhetorical way in which he couched Whig political ideology in millennial terms.[45] John Adams's diary entry for Sunday, 23 April 1773, signals Cooper's method:

> Heard Dr. Chauncy in the Morning and Dr. Cooper this Afternoon. Dr. Cooper was up[on] Rev. 12.9. And the great Dragon was cast out, that old Serpent called the Devil and Satan, which deceiveth the whole World: he was cast out into the Earth and his

Angells were cast out with him. Q[uery]. Whether the Dr. had not some political Allusions in the Choice of this Text.[46]

The query had to have been for Adams an ironic, private joke: Cooper was privy to the same sensational news that Adams, Hancock, and some other staunch Whigs of Boston had learned—that Thomas Hutchinson had been deceiving the people of Boston and sending negative reports of their behavior to England, as revealed in the newly received packet of letters Franklin had mailed Cushing.

From the time of the French and Indian War Cooper had used biblical texts to make political statements. In fact, his conflation of political and religious ideology had begun in the 1750s, when he asserted that his ancestors transplanted themselves into the wilds of America because they had been "smitten with a Love of Liberty, and possessed with an uncommon Reverence to the Dictates of Conscience."[47] Cooper's avowed social ideal of religious and civil liberty became his persuasive equation of piety and Whiggery in his sermons.[48] *Liberty* would have been a term well liked by his elite parishioners, most of them representatives of Boston's richest mercantile interests.

Little wonder, then, that Cooper was dubbed "Silver-Tongued Sam."[49] He was so popular as to require denunciation in at least two well-known political ballads. One, a version of *The Boston Ministers* (1774), alludes to Cooper's political activity:

> There's Cooper too, a doctor true,
>   Is sterling in his way;
> To Jerry Seed, all are agreed,
>   He well be likened may.
> In politics, he all the tricks,
>   Doth wonderously ken,
> In's country's cause and for her laws,
>   Above most mortal men.[50]

Thomas Bolton more viciously attacked Cooper, implying that Cooper too clearly spoke politics while in the pulpit:

> He, prostituting his religion,
> Turns a dispenser of sedition;
> And to the greedy, gaping million,
> For holy writ, deals out rebellion;
> His sacred function quite forsaking,
> Smells profit in oration making.[51]

Cooper's popularity as a preacher made his political bias inimical to British sympathizers. The combination of piety and Whig ideology produced a persuasive rhetoric hard to discredit. In fact, their inability to discredit Cooper so frustrated Tories like Peter Oliver that Cooper became the object of their unremitting hatred. "[A]s the *Boston* Clergy were esteemed by the others as an

Order of Deities," Oliver wrote, "so they were greatly influenced by them." Oliver justified his own behavior toward the patriots by writing for a sympathetic loyalist audience that:

> Dr. *Cooper* was a young Man—very polite in his Manners—of a general Knowledge—not deep in his Profession, but very deep in the black Art. His behavior in Company was very insinuating especially among the fair Sex. . . . No Man could, with a better Grace, utter the Word of *God* from his Mouth, & at the same Time keep a two edged Dagger concealed in his Hand. His Tongue was Butter & Oil, but under it was the Poison of Asps. . . . The Fluency of his Tongue & the Ease of his Manners atoned with some for all his Dissimulation; for his Manners were such, that he was always agreeable to the politest Company, who were unacquainted with his real Character; & he could descend from them to mix privately with the Rabble, in their nightly seditious Associations.[52]

Oliver's denunciation of Cooper contains some interesting points about the popular perceptions the minister created among his audience. Cooper evidently did insist upon the possibility of reconciliation, even until just before the war, while seeming to have understood that war was imminent—and not necessarily undesirable.[53] He was so respected as to have been offered the presidency of Harvard in February 1774, an honor he did not accept.[54] In addition, Cooper was evidently a favorite among the ladies and was welcomed in the most elite and the poorest circles.[55] Such an esteemed man was indeed a persuasive, powerful foe of the Tory leadership. Cooper preached that the dictates of conscience had called the colonists' ancestors to a love of liberty and to free enterprise; such preaching no doubt impressed the audience at Brattle Street. Given Cooper's social, political, and professional renown; given the probability of his having known the latest news from England because of his friendship with Franklin and the colonial sympathizers there; given his popularity with both sexes—Cooper is likely the character fictionalized as Jedediah the priest in *The First Book of the American Chronicles of the Times*.

* * *

If Samuel Cooper is Jedediah the priest, then Aminadab, of the tribe of Jedediah (1.47), is most likely William Cooper, Samuel's older brother. In the satire, Aminadab ponders situations just as William Cooper, town clerk and clerk of the Boston Committee of Correspondence, evidently pondered comments from meetings, deciding whether or not to put them in the record. He seems to have recorded information selectively, and was especially careful about what was recorded from the meetings of the Committee of Correspondence. And as a patriot agitator, he often virtually controlled the town meetings.[56]

One of William Cooper's more interesting endeavors relates to the Solemn League and Covenant, which originated with the Boston Committee of Correspondence. William Cooper, knowing the country people were more inclined toward open resistance, suggested that the committee send the Solemn League and Covenant to the back country to gain support. In a letter written 22 July 1774, John Andrews (a member of Samuel Cooper's Brattle Street congregation and a prominent merchant who would have liked other measures taken than boycotting) peevishly reported:

> I made some observations on the solemn *League and Covenant*, which I had not then [June 22] seen, as it was not known to be in being in this town (but by the few who promoted it) till near a month after it had been circulated through the country: in which time it went through whole towns with the greatest avidity, every adult of both sexes putting their names to it, saving a very few. It was sent out in printed copies by the Clerk of the Committee, W. Cooper, who accompanied it with a letter intimating that the measure was in general adopted here, whereas upon enquiry I can't find that a single person in the town has signed it. . . .[57]

William Cooper was a clever, formidable opponent of the Tory factions. By September 1774, he had become so prominent a member of the Whig contingent that he was included in the list of those "authors" of provincial miseries whom a newspaper letter urged the redcoats to plunder. Others on the list included Samuel Cooper, Charles Chauncy, James Bowdoin, John Hancock, Thomas Cushing, Samuel Adams, and the publishers of the *Gazette* and the *Spy*.[58] In 1780 the Cooper brothers received this denunciation in London's *Political Register:*

> William Cooper . . . is one of the greatest knaves and most inveterate rebels in New England. He is a very hot-headed man, and constantly urged the most violent measures. He was prompted secretly by his brother, the Reverend Samuel Cooper, who, though a minister of peace and to all outward appearances a meek and heavenly man, yet was one of the chief instruments in stirring up the people to take arms.[59]

The Cooper brothers, influential opponents of Britain's coercive measures, would have been an apt twosome to fictionalize in a patriot propagandist satire. The brothers' prominence, both civil and religious, won them the approbation of their Whig and the opprobrium of their Tory contemporaries.

* * *

The identity of Jeremiah, another central character in the satire, is more difficult to establish. Jeremiah makes an address in only one section of *The First Book of the American Chronicles of the Times* (2.27ff.). The appeals of this address create interest in his character. Here, Jeremiah tells of his vision, a vision similar to Peter's in Acts 10, except that Peter's four wild beasts are Jeremiah's duty-gatherers and searchers. Jeremiah, like his biblical namesake, warns of the destruction that will occur if the present crisis remains unresolved.

Perhaps Jeremiah represents the Reverend Dr. Charles Chauncy, pastor of Boston's First Church. At a time when most ministers preached jeremiads to their congregations, Chauncy stood out as a staunch believer in the possibility of a civil millennium. Shipton reports, for instance, that Chauncy "extolled the Puritans, decried the sins of his own time, denounced balls, and demanded sumptuary legislation."[60] Chauncy lamented his degenerate times and urged the present generation to strive to replace the mighty generation passing away.[61] But Chauncy's theology taught that God delivers only those who are deserving.[62] The people deserved deliverance during the Stamp Act crisis, Chauncy preached in *"the good News from a far Country."*[63] And they were likely to be deserving again, delivered again, at some time in the future. Nathan Hatch explains Chauncy's civil millennialism:

> In marked contrast to the apolitical millennial hopes of Jonathan Edwards, which had been based on the success of the revival, civil millennialism advanced freedom as the cause of God, defined the primary enemy as the Antichrist of civil oppression rather than of formal religion, traced the myths of its past through political developments rather than through the vital religion of the forefathers, and turned its vision toward privileges of Britons rather than to a heritage exclusive to New England.[64]

By the 1770s the force of civil millennialism had been brought to bear against England itself. Ministers identified England's plan to enslave the colonies with Satan's continuing conspiracy against God's people. They detected the corruption of placemen in the growth of arbitrary power, the malice of Satan in the threat of standing armies.[65]

Chauncy believed that New England's deliverance from the sinful powers of Britain would eventually come. Indeed, he saw the unity of the colonies during the prewar crisis as God's miraculous gift to a deserving people. Chauncy's sermons of 1774 continually alluded to signs of God's favor. Jane Mecom wrote to Franklin in November of that year, "Doctor Chauncy says we have all redy had miracles wrought in our favour won of which is the Uniteing of the Colonies in such a maner, another the Extroydnary fruitfull seasons and Bounty of our friends and looks on it as a token of Gods Design to deliver us out of all our trobles."[66] Chauncy's starkly plain but persuasive approach brought him this comment in *The Boston Ministers:*

> That fine preacher, called a teacher,
>   Of Old Brick Church the first,
> Regards no grace, to men in place,
>   And is by tories curst.
> At young and old, he'll rave and scold,
>   And is, in things of state,
> A zealous Whig, then Wilkes more big,
>   In Church a tyrant Great.[68]

Chauncy's sermons lamenting the Boston seige and Britain's stranglehold on Boston's Great Neck, in addition to his pleas for deliverance, make him a fitting Jeremiah for *The First Book of the American Chronicles of the Times.*

* * *

The counterpart for the fictionalized character Obadiah is as difficult to establish as that for Jeremiah. Obadiah appears in several parts of the *American Chronicles,* but in only some of them does he play an important role. He appears with the selectmen (2.57) and in a section in which he describes the inherited possession of New England (3.14ff.) after the manner of Deuteronomy 8.7. His most humorous appearance occurs in chapters 3 and 4, when he, Jedediah, and Aminadab visit his friend, Mother Carey. In a section full of scurrility and sexual puns, Mother Carey invites Jedediah (recall that Samuel Cooper was especially popular with women)—alone—into her house. As Mother Carey had been *his*—not Jedediah's—friend, Obadiah becomes "exceedingly jealous, howbeit he held his peace." Mumbling in his rage, Obadiah is only somewhat appeased when Mother Carey finally admits him and Aminadab to her table. He grumblingly leaves her house at the end of this section (4.25).

That Obadiah appears among the selectmen, concerns himself with the possessions of the country, and is jealous of Jedediah's interest in Mother Carey (Obadiah's friend, after all) might mean that Obadiah is a fictional representation of John Hancock, rich Boston merchant, member of the Brattle Street congregation, and political agitator. Until about May 1773, Hancock's political sentiments had seemed to vacillate between pro-crown and moderate patriot support. A successful merchant, he surely realized that a break with Britain would result in his own financial loss. Hancock's shrewdness, in the early 1770s especially, seems to have been unparalleled.[68] The deciding factor for Hancock's taking the patriot side seems to have been the letter packet Franklin sent to the colonies. Terrifically angered by Hutchinson's duplicity, Hancock became the agent by which the letters were exposed.[69] Thereafter, Hancock became active with the Committee of Correspondence, publicly espousing patriot action.

Hancock could be represented by Obadiah on several counts. First, Hancock was openly interested in the activities of the selectmen once the Hutchinson or Whately letters had become common knowledge, and he was especially driven to action during the powder scare. Second, his interest in colonial "possessions" relates to Obadiah's speech (3.14ff.) about the colonial inheritance. In fact, this section, along with Obadiah's other speeches, perhaps reflects Hancock's immensely popular oration spoken on the anniversary of the Boston Massacre, 5 March 1774. In the *Oration* Hancock denounced the Tea Act as sheer tyranny, exhorting his listeners "that, if necessary ye fight, and even die for the prosperity of our Jerusalem."[70] Obadiah's speeches contain similar messages, perhaps by design. Chapter 3 of the satire, which contains Obadiah's longest statement about the colonial inheritance, was not published in Philadelphia until December 1774; Hancock's *Oration* had been frequently reprinted—two editions in Boston by early April and editions in Newport, New Haven, and Philadelphia shortly thereafter—in pamphlets and newspapers.[71]

In addition, the episode concerning Mother Carey might have been an amusing comment on Hancock's relations with a woman who was about a dozen years his senior. A woman named Dorcas Griffiths ran a spirits store conveniently located on Hancock's Wharf. About Hancock's attentions to her Shipton asserts, "This choice of a mistress solely for comfort and convenience was so typical of the man who could have had any unmarried woman in Boston to wife, that it caused considerable amusement."[72] Shipton reports that Hancock left her to the regulars around 1771. If the name *Mother Carey* in the 1770s could have indicated a woman who ran a house of prostitution—as it did by 1807[73]—then the use in *American Chronicles* of Mother Carey and Obadiah's attachment and jealousy could be an amusing glance at Hancock and his friend, Dorcas Griffiths. The possibility, at least, must have afforded considerable amusement to the contemporary audience, if not to Hancock.

• • •

The character Phineas clearly represents Israel Putnam. Phineas, described in *The First Book of the American Chronicles of the Times* as having a ruddy face and warm disposition, is the "captain of the host, a mighty man, and a warrior from his youth." Moreover, he "killed four she bears, and slew three giants . . . in single combat" and "was a captain of old at the seige of Louisbourg" (3.27–28). The last is surely a reference to Israel Putnam's reputed, even then legendary, demonstration of martial ability.

One of the earliest legends associated with Putnam is that in the winter of 1742–1743 Putnam killed a large wolf in her den.[74] Then, during the French and Indian Wars, Putnam evidently had been captured in August 1758 by the Indians—who were preparing to burn him at the stake—and was rescued. By the 1770s, popular stories about "Old Put" abounded, and his heroism was the stuff of legend. In August 1774, Putnam drove a herd of 125 sheep into the hungry town of Boston. Putnam's popularity as an American hero made him, like Phineas, an appropriate symbol of patriot valor.

• • •

Finally, two less prominent characters are perhaps identifiable. Caleb, mentioned only three times in the *American Chronicles*, probably represents Joseph Warren. When news gets out about the seizure of powder, "Caleb and his brethren, ten men in number, were sent as spies" (1.42), and Caleb appears among the selectmen who help calm down the people (2.57). Caleb's actions resemble Warren's in that when a crowd of people had gathered to question the seizure of the powder and to demand the resignations of the members of the newly named Mandamus Council, the Boston Committee of Correspondence, under the leadership of Joseph Warren, headed off violence.[75]

If Joseph Warren is represented by Caleb, then "Othniel, Caleb's younger brother," could be Joseph Warren's younger brother John. Othniel's name appears among the names of the selectmen who quelled the people's fears when the powder was seized. Although Caleb's and Othniel's actions are few in *The First Book of the American Chronicles of the Times*, it seems likely that the two characters represent the Warren brothers.

• • •

Most readers of the *The First Book of the American Chronicles of the Times* have agreed that much of the fun of reading the satire comes from the wish to link the actions of noted patriots with the fictional representations in the text. Conclusive identifications can perhaps never be established; there are no "conclusive" identifications possible. Part of the fun for contemporary readers who were entirely familiar with patriot activities must have been guessing—with too few details fully to ascertain—the characters' identities. Indeed, part of the effect of the parodic satire is possible precisely because the audience could be expected to search out the biblical analogues for the present agitators.

Contemporary Bible Genres

Biblical characters and events had long been used for literary and political purposes. The classic among works drawing on the Bible for characters and events is John Dryden's *Absalom and Achitophel* (1681), which uses the rebellion of Absalom against his father, King David, as told in 2 Samuel 13–18, to recount its remarkable parallel in the illegitimate Monmouth's attempt to gain the throne from his father, King Charles II. By finding the biblical analogue for the contemporary situation, Dryden could elicit in his reader a sense of the importance of the events at hand. Such use of the Bible to relate contemporary events to Bible history was common from the Renaissance.

Parodies of the Bible differ from works like *Absalom and Achitophel* in that while developing a biblical allegory or parable of the contemporary events, they evoke biblical narration as well. In most cases, the texts that appropriate biblical narration to make implied critical comment on contemporary social and political situations in order to hint at their correction can most accurately be called parodic satires. See the Significance section below.

The appropriation of biblical texts seems to have been a technique adopted by the colonists after it had begun in England. Horace Walpole included an early political satire narrated in a biblical manner in a letter to Horace Mann, 14 July 1742.[76] "The Lesson for the Day" satirizes the men who sought preferment after the resignation of Sir Robert Walpole in February 1742. Of this satire Walpole later wrote, "This piece, with a very few additions, was the original of a numberless quantity of the same kind, which were published upon all subjects for a year or two."[77] Of course, the truth of this statement is difficult to assess.

But parodic satires in the form of biblical narrations indeed seemed to have appeared with remarkable regularity after 1742. Trevor Colbourn has pointed out, "Probably the most successful of English works reprinted in America was the *Chronicle of the Kings of England*, a curious Biblical parody."[78] This *Chronicle* seems to have been first reprinted in America in Newport, Rhode Island, in 1744.[79] The first biblical parodic satire Charles Evans recorded (but did not reprint—perhaps because it is not extant) was published in 1746: John Anderson's *The Book of the Chronicles of his Royal Highness, William Duke of Cumberland: Being an Account of the Rise and Progress of the Present Rebellion* (Evans no. 5732).[80] Another early example was probably written by Stephen Hopkins or his party in Rhode Island, *The Fall of Samuel the Squomicutite, and the Overthrow of the Sons of Gideon*, an attack on Gideon Wanton and Samuel Ward, both of whom Hopkins considered insufficiently patriotic.[81] In 1766, a satire popular in London appeared in the colonial papers. This work, the "Book of America," satirized the events surrounding the Stamp Act. Albert C. Matthews has shown that "The Book of America" was widely reprinted and perhaps became the inspiration for a satire of less importance, "The Book of Harvard," which appeared in September 1766. "The Book of Harvard" satirized the steward's persistent serving of bad butter in commons.[82]

Printers in the colonies widely reprinted these and other biblical parodic satires in local newspapers. One example is John Holt's publication in September 1772 of several "Chapters of Isaac the Scribe," a satire on the family of Jacob Franks, a prominent New York merchant, in his *New York Journal or General Advertiser*.[83] Parodic satires in the form of biblical narratives, then, were well-known diversions—on both public and private themes—in the colonies long before Leacock began writing *The First Book of the American Chronicles of the Times* in 1774.

Bible hoaxes were popular as well. Hoaxes differ from parodic satires largely because they offer such close biblical renderings that they can be mistaken for actual Bible texts. Benjamin Franklin, John Leacock's relative by marriage, was fond of his own biblical hoaxes, commonly known as "A Parable against Persecution" and "A Parable on Brotherly Love."[84] These two hoaxes imperceptibly veil, according to Franklin's ruse, specific political commentary on contemporary events with carefully contrived Bible-like language. Both are true parables, then, not parodic satires. Written around 1755, roughly two years before Franklin went to England with copies of it, "A Parable against Persecution" follows the style of the King James Bible. As a ruse, Franklin enjoyed reading the parable in company as part of Genesis and then encouraging his listeners to comment on the text. Leacock could easily have witnessed such a reading (if indeed he did not himself read the manuscript), for he was part of the family circle that included brothers-in-law David Hall and James Read. Leacock certainly knew Franklin and his hoaxes and probably enjoyed both of these works.

Biblical narrations, both as satires and as hoaxes, continued to be produced through the end of the century. Leacock's *American Chronicles* might have influenced Philadelphian Francis Hopkinson's "A Prophecy," written about

1776 but not then published. In "A Prophecy" Hopkinson pushed for independence using biblical diction that parodies Old Testament phraseology.[85] The "Chapters of Isaac the Scribe" (originally printed by Holt in the *New York Journal*) were evidently printed in pamphlet form in 1775 (Evans no. 14461).[86] Nuel Bostwick's *The First Book of Chronicles. The Political War in Ballston* (1799; Evans no. 35223) seems to have been one of the last parodic satires written as a biblical narration.[87]

Other Bible genres used for political messages and popular around the time of the Revolution include catechisms and Bible commentaries. *A Ministerial Catechise, Suitable to be Learned by All Modern Provincial Governors, Pensioners, Placemen, &c. Dedicated to T[homas]. H[utchinson]., Esq.* (1771; Evans no. 12128) exaggerated the baseness of bought loyalty and burlesqued sacred obligations.[88] Leacock's parody might have influenced Oliver Noble's *Some Strictures upon the Sacred Story Recorded in the Book of Esther, Shewing the Power and Oppression of State Ministers tending to the Ruin and Destruction of God's People* (1775; Evans no. 14352), a commentary that worked out the parallels between the biblical Book of Esther and contemporary ministerial conspiracies.[89] Noble's parallels were strikingly similar to Leacock's: Haman is Lord North; the Jews are the colonists; and Mordecai is Franklin. Clearly, the Bible proved a rich source of material for writers interested in denouncing the social and political evils of England's rule in America during the latter part of the eighteenth century. Leacock's *The First Book of the American Chronicles of the Times* is one in a tradition of biblical takeoffs popular during his lifetime.

The Significance of Leacock's *American Chronicles*

Twentieth-century readers might be inclined to think that the eighteenth-century popularity of works like *The First Book of the American Chronicles of the Times* arose because—to phrase the conception in the broadest possible terms—in an age characterized by enlightened deism the Bible was a worn-out text, a text more the butt of humor than the source of prophetic truth for men.[90] As the brief survey of Bible genres above indicates, however, the Bible provided eighteenth-century writers with ready formulas for conveying belief and instruction and/or satire (and instruction). It is surely accurate to say that the Bible was a good vehicle for moral, social, and political commentary precisely because it was a well-known and often cited text. In fact, people during the eighteenth century differed little from their sixteenth- and seventeenth-century counterparts in their attitudes of praise and blame—one might say, ambivalence—toward the Bible and biblical exegesis. The significance of Leacock's biblical parodic satire can perhaps best be assessed in the general context of the millennial expectations—prominent during the sixteenth, seventeenth, and eighteenth centuries—surrounding the Reformation in England, the settlement of the colonies, the rise (and fall) of Oliver Cromwell, and the ideological turbulence in the colonies just preceding the American Revolution.

From the time of the Reformation, when writers and preachers searched the prophetic texts of the Bible for explanation and justification for the break with the Roman church, through the eighteenth century, prominent intellectuals preoccupied themselves with the significance of biblical prophecy in the determination of present and future events.[91] This is not to say that interest in the relationship between biblical prophecy and history began in the sixteenth century or that renewed interest in prophecy occurred in the sixteenth century only because of the Reformation debate. Rather, the debate brought about a distinguishable Protestant version of prophecy, particularly of the Book of Revelation, a version insisting that the threat of Papal and Roman Catholic domination were signified by the legion of Antichrist in the Books of Daniel and Revelation.[92] In the Protestant interpretation of events, the Catholic church became a dominant figure among the beasts of Revelation that signaled the apocalypse and Christ's second coming.[93] For a culture having what Paul J. Korshin has called a "typological propensity," nothing could carry more significance.[94]

Intense speculation about the arrival of the apocalypse continued after the Renaissance, and it was carried on not only by Dissenters or Puritans but by orthodox Anglican churchmen as well. The Cambridge Platonists in the 1670s and 80s, the French Prophets (Camisards) in the early 1700s, John Wesley and his followers in the 1740s—all were convinced, Korshin says, "that the signs of the times spelled apocalypse."[95] In fact, many intellectuals of the English Enlightenment engaged in the millenarian exegesis of Scripture, "abetted," again to quote Korshin, "by a steady stream of fundamentalist Christian, Jewish, and—in Britain's new empire—Islamic visionaries."[96] Prophetic signs of the times became the preoccupation for those of any religious persuasion.

Millenarian activities within a Puritan frame of reference became most intense from the 1640s to the 1660s, partly caused by the increased settlement in the American colonies, and partly, by the rise (and fall) of Oliver Cromwell. The Puritans who came to Massachusetts Bay evidently saw their settlement in Boston as the *telos* and converging point of secular and sacred history, the fulfillment of the scriptural prophecy that placed them on a level with the ancient Israelites. They were new Israelites in a new Canaan. In a settlement they believed authorized by God, these Puritans saw a new era beginning for God's elect, an era to which they had been assigned—as scriptural prophecy promised—the central role in the necessary progress of salvation.[97] Indeed, even the physical, institutional, and ideological difficulties they faced were taken as signs of their election; time, to these Puritans, was drawing to its close, and the difficulties were signs that Christ was undertaking his final conflict with Satan.[98]

And, to many Puritans, Oliver Cromwell signified the new Christ. Millenarian typology of the 1640s and 1650s, as evidenced most clearly in Andrew

Marvell's *The First Anniversary of the Government of O.C.* (1655), identified the Lord Protector with the Old Testament types of Christ (especially Moses, Joshua, and David) and so insisted that Cromwell himself typified Christ—both Christ the Savior and Christ the deliverer of the world from Antichrist.[99] Cromwell's actions were popularly construed as a prefiguration of Christ's action at the time of the apocalypse; Cromwell's death, as an opportunity for a further covenant and renewed peace, the interlude of stillness before *the* apocalyptic event.[100]

The New England Puritans staunchly supported the English Revolution in both prayer and action, engaging in fast days, in bans of royalist support, and in the revolutionary effort itself.[101] As Alfred F. Young has shown, upon Cromwell's defeat, he "entered the popular tradition, where he was stored in folklore—in legend and place lore—for more than a century."[102] To have fought in Cromwell's army was a sure distinction, and the appearance of the regicides Goffe, Whalley, and Dixwell in New England provided welcome sources for popular legend there.[103] In New England more than in the other colonies, Cromwell's importance reigned supreme in the popular imagination in two distinct ways: enthusiastic religion and a subterranean folk tradition that saw Cromwell as the avenging savior of the elect.[104] In addition to naming their children after him, the common people of New England popularized Cromwell's memory by using his first name in stories about him and by naming localities after him.[105] While their counterparts in England witnessed the fading glory of Cromwell, New Englanders—especially in the non-elite culture—kept Cromwell alive as a folk hero.

In England, Puritan attitudes toward Cromwell shifted as the eighteenth century began. The theme of Cromwell the usurper, Cromwell the tyrant began to take hold, perhaps as a result of the influence of republican Edmund Ludlow's memoirs.[106] A costly and ill-kept English standing army was seen as the legacy of Oliver Cromwell. According to Catherine Macaulay, the Puritans' favorite historian, the Civil War and Interregnum were to be remembered as one the most heroic periods of English history, although Oliver Cromwell, "a master in all powers of grimace and the arts of hypocrisy," was not a noble figure, because he managed to dispense with a people's Parliament and establish instead a despotism with a standing army.[107] Coupled with the denigration of the royalist pamphleteers, these complaints from would-have-been Cromwell supporters entered the political tradition in England and began to be entertained by the elite in the colonies.

To the New England elite, Cromwell's greatest legacy was the hateful presence of a British standing army in Boston. In *Observations on the Act of Parliament Commonly Called the Boston Port-Bill* (Boston, 1774), Josiah Quincy said that Cromwell, like Caesar, had enslaved his country with armies "stationed in the very bowels of the land."[108] John Adams had noted in his diary on 10 September 1761, that "Oliver was successful but not prudent nor honest nor lawdable nor imitable."[109] "In the Commonwealth political tradition, which New England's leaders of the revolutionary era adopted," Alfred Young has commented, "Cromwell was anathema."[110]

But the leaders of the revolutionary agitation were not the people whom they were trying to persuade to agitate. Cromwell's attitudes and his political measures might have been questionable to the elite; they were not questionable in non-elite culture. And, as Alfred Young has shown, even the elite had a "sneaking admiration for Cromwell," although its public stance was one of intolerance for him.[111] Thus, two conceptions of Cromwell existed side by side in New England, probably in the colonies generally. On the one hand, Cromwell was the hero of the folk; on the other, Cromwell was the tyrant of the oppressed. To have propagandized against Cromwell in exactly the media—broadsides, pamphlets, and newspapers—used to persuade the non-elite culture to resist England would clearly have defeated the purposes of the elite revolutionary leaders in New England and throughout the colonies. In fact, in the propaganda of the elite that seems to have been intended for the common people, negative commentary about Cromwell is largely absent. The elite culture capitalized on the popular conception of Cromwell as avenging saviour.[112]

The elite could do so because of Cromwell's survival not only in popular folk ways but in enthusiastic religion. Millennialism was not absent in New England in the eighteenth century. In fact, the Great Awakening of the 1740s brought about the fairly cohesive rise of an evangelical, crusading spirit that prepared Americans for revolutions in their social and political affairs as signs of their place in salvation history.[113] To Jonathan Edwards, the revivals were "the dawning, or at least a prelude, of that glorious work of God, so often foretold in Scripture, which in the progress and issue of it shall renew the world of mankind." Edwards had "great longings for the advancement of Christ's kingdom in the world" and was "eager to read the public news-letters, mainly for that end, to see if I could not find some news favorable to the interest of religion in the world."[114] New England millennial enthusiasts generally accepted Edwards's postmillennialism—that the spirit of Christ would be present during the millennium but that the Second Coming would occur afterward—and placed themselves in the position of helping usher in the kingdom of Christ.[115]

The non-elite culture adapted the Lord Protector of a century before as the renewed signifier for this new world, the sign of Christ's second coming. The eighteenth-century common people got Cromwell with a difference—the millennial enthusiasm of the 1740s. To the enthusiasts, even the earthquakes of 1727 and 1755 signified their coming glory.[116] According to Revelation, enthusiasts reasoned, the saints were to undergo many sufferings before their final deliverance. In this view, the Revolutionary War was just another setback assigned to God's people.

The revolutionary elite culture capitalized on these popular conceptions.

Although members of the elite themselves might not have thought Cromwell "imitable" (*vide* John Adams), although they might not themselves have experienced religious enthusiasm, they understood well their constituents. Cromwell became a central symbol; the American Revolution, the central cause. In this context, it is not at all surprising that John Leacock's *The First Book of the American Chronicles of the Times* was so immensely popular. The parodic satire used the ideology (millennialism) and folk heroes (Cromwell and others) popular among the non-elite groups, yet it offered these popular appeals in such a way as to effect a satiric stance perceivable by an elite audience.

Thus the form of the *American Chronicles* as parodic satire assured its popularity with elite and non-elite alike.[117] The double-voicing available in its form as biblical parodic satire replicated the double vision found in the elite and non-elite cultures. As biblical parody, the satire offered in its form alone a textual model of what the enthusiastic non-elite culture was doing—appropriating the Bible text to create a new text. That is, just as the parodic form of the *American Chronicles* was a re-constitution of biblical texts in the formulation of a new text, the *American Chronicles*, so was the enthusiastic New England Puritan millennialist version of American salvation history a re-constitution of biblical history. While the elite culture could find a satiric effect from the parodic narrative, the non-elite culture could find validation in the re-constitution of the Bible text. Such a double-voicing is especially apparent in the section of the *American Chronicles* that treats Oliver Cromwell. I will discuss that section after a brief consideration of the question of genre.

The elite/non-elite double vision noted above is an effect of what Linda Hutcheon calls the paradox of parody.[118] Perhaps because parody was often used for satiric ends during the eighteenth century, the word *parody* connotes to many readers today a negatively critical or satiric or mocking effect. But Samuel Johnson's 1755 definition of parody relates it more to imitation than to satire: "A kind of writing, in which the words of an author or his thoughts are taken, and by a slight change adapted to some new purpose."[119] Parody, then, works within a set of norms while transgressing and refunctioning them.[120] Biblical parody works within the text of the Bible (the "target" text) in order to transgress it and offer a new text, a re-constituted text. The re-constituted text is not necessarily a ridiculing imitation of the target; rather, the ironic inversion of the new text can be playful as well as belittling, critically constructive as well as destructive.[121] Parody is simply, as Hutcheon has phrased it, "repetition with difference"; its repetition of the old and re-constitution into the new, its carnivalesque inversions, are emancipating.[122]

Because *The First Book of the American Chronicles of the Times* offers a social and political message, I have called it a biblical parodic satire. The aim of parody is intramural; that of satire, extramural—social or moral.[123] The *American Chronicles* clearly parodies the Bible, but it parodies that text in order to re-constitute it for implied social and political commentary. Its extramural aim takes the *American Chronicles* into the realm of satire; the *American Chronicles* "aims at something outside the text, but . . . employs parody as a vehicle to achieve its satiric or corrective end"—Hutcheon's definition of parodic satire.[124] The target of the parody is the Bible; the targets of the parodic satire are England and the New England non-elite—both of which have oppressive, tyrannic, and self-aggrandizing agendas.

The First Book of the American Chronicles of the Times is clearly anti-British for both the elite and non-elite cultures in the colonies. The English are denigrated as luxury-loving, virtue-mocking, vainly militaristic, superstitious, papacy-worshiping scoundrels whose leader in America (Thomas Gage) deserves to be afraid of his own shadow. American leaders like Benjamin Franklin and Israel Putnam, on the other hand, are celebrated as heroes of steadfast virtue, strength, and intelligence. The parodic satire clearly targets British sympathizers.

But the *American Chronicles* wields a two-edged sword. Throughout the satire, the people of Boston assert the rightness of the cause—especially with regard to the protection of their goods in the land of milk and honey—and they offer, as justification, biblical analogues for their actions. (Implication: they are self-important, militant ideologues.) They rely on Mother Carey, a witch, for aid in the struggle. (Implication: they are superstitious.) They use flattery when it suits their purposes. (Implication: they are vain and hypocritical.) In other words, in their militant zeal for Revolution (to bring about the millennium), the fictionalized Bostonites are not much different from their English counterparts.

The satire becomes most clear at the climactic moment—marked by the key parodic devices of juxtaposition and addition—when Cromwell is raised from the dead. In a nearly apocalyptic fit upon Cromwell's appearance, "Jedediah spake, and lifted up his hands and eyes, and said":

> O how highly favored are we thy sons, that it be permitted that thou, our great Lord and mighty Protector, regardest his children, who hatest hypocrisy and dissimulation, whose conscience is void of offence, who refused an earthly crown that thou mightest be rewarded with a crown of glory, who art ambitious only for the glory of the King of Kings; thou whose consummate fortitude, magnanimity and prudence, whose great and divine talents were bestowed from above, to answer wise purposes and happy events, how didst thou raise the fading glory and dying reputation of the British nation, beyond the highest pitch of Roman greatness; the heads of kings and princes were but as snow balls in thine hands, and thou hustled powers, principalities, and kingdoms as in a cap; thou became the dread and terror of the nations round about; thou swayed the sceptre of this terrestrial universe, and held the balance of power in thine own hands, thou broughtest true religion to the highest pitch, and banished enthusiasm, fanaticism, high church bigotry, popish superstition, and pretenders to saintship, out of the land; thou shook his holiness's hair, made the tripple crown of the great dragon to totter, thou madest the papal cap to fall off his shoulders, and made thereof a carpet for the soles of thy shoes, and left him as bare as an unfledged woodpecker; thou suffered not the haughty king of France to enjoy his boasted vain title, but permitted him to be called only the simple French king; the invincible proud

> Spaniard thou humbled in the dust, and made their donships, Don Falsey Benabio, and Don Diego Surly Phiz, their ministers, as submissive as spaniels; thou despised their treasure, their silver and their gold, and sunk their galleons in the depths of the sea; the sly Hogan Mogans of the United Provinces trembled at thy nod, they besought thy friendship, and their high Mightynesses became the poor and distressed states; the strong holds and impenetrable castles of the piratical Algerines became but as sport and pastime in thine hands, and the ships of all the nations thou made to lower their pride, pay homage, and bow down to thy all conquering flag; thou settest up whatsoever thou pleasest, and pullest down whomsoever thou wilt. (4.12)

Cromwell, "not proof to flattery," broadly smiled on Jedediah, for he "rejoiced to hear his own actions and great atchievements praised and extolled, even unto the skies" (4.13). The non-elite audience probably found in this exaggerated, apocalyptic image of Cromwell (in full battle armor!) the kind of praise they popularly set up in their own folk portraits of the Lord Protector during Pope's Day celebrations.[125] The exaggeration, in fact, would not have been much different from that used of Cromwell in mummers' plays.[126] The Cromwell section offered the non-elite culture a re-functioning of the Bible that added a vitality to their millennial enthusiasm.

But to an elite audience familiar with the Commonwealth political tradition, this exaggerated portrait surely revealed the expected Cromwell-the-usurper theme. To those who did not see Cromwell as the antetype of Christ at the Second Coming, Cromwell would have been perceived here as proud and self-important, vain and egotistical. The events narrated stress the despotic militarism of Cromwell's policies—to the elite, the reminder that Cromwell did, in his day, what the New England populace in the 1770s claimed old England was doing. The elite audience would have enjoyed the implied Whig party line that Cromwell—like George III—imposed his own sense of justice on all those around him, denying their rights in the assertion of his own. The elite audience surely understood the implied warning in Leacock's *American Chronicles*—little different from the one Franklin was known to have given—that both New England and old must act with reasonableness and moderation. It was a warning peculiarly fitting to the Quaker city.

John Leacock, a merchant and surely a member of the colonial elite culture, understood the necessity both for agitation and for preventing mob action. Targeting the non-elite followers of folk tradition and enthusiastic religion, *The First Book of the American Chronicles of the Times* satirizes the extremist behavior found in New England and old. It reveals in John Leacock the ability "of elites to capitalise on what they perceived to be existing popular veneration of a particular patriot symbol."[127] In celebrating Franklin and Cromwell alike, *The First Book of the American Chronicles of the Times* offered a message familiar to both its elite and its non-elite audience; its double-voiced parodic form was its own sign of the times.

Parodic forms tend to prosper in periods of cultural sophistication that enable parodists to rely on the competence of the receiver of the parody.[128] The eighteenth century in America offered such cultural sophistication. The century was marked by an ideological ambivalence, with its competing millenarian and deistic interpretations of human history. The double-voicing of the parodic forms that flourished during the eighteenth century indicates the general ambivalence perceived by many intellectuals. It has been suggested that interest in parody diminished after the eighteenth century because of the aesthetic assumptions behind the Romantic movement, which held parody in disrepute as the imitative enemy of originality and creativity.[129] Perhaps in this present age of exhaustion, an aesthetic plurality will emerge that will free the theorists and the historians of American literature and culture alike to the vitality, indeed the "emancipation," of parodic satires written at the time of the American Revolution.

The Printings

The best indication of the contemporary popularity of Leacock's *The First Book of the American Chronicles of the Times* is the number of pamphlet and newspaper reprintings it received, especially of the early chapters. Each of the six chapters was first printed by Benjamin Towne in Philadelphia. The following table, adapted from information reported by Bowman,[130] indicates the numbers and locations of the printings of each chapter:

Chapter	Philadelphia Printing	Evans Number
1	October 1774	Boston (5) Newbern (1) Norwich (1) Providence (1) Salem (1)
2	November 1774	Boston (5) Norwich (1) Providence (1) Salem (2)
3	December 1774	Boston (4) Norwich (1) Providence (1)
4	January 1775	Boston (4) Norwich (1) Providence (1)
5	February 1775	Boston (3) Norwich (1)
6	February 1775	[no reprintings located]

Although the sixth chapter, like all the others, closes with "[To be continued.]," it was evidently the last chapter of the *American Chronicles* to be printed. Many considerations might account for the diminishing number of reprintings of the satire. After the meeting of the First Continental Congress, the colonies began a concerted effort to prepare for war. Leacock might himself have decided that direct oratorical appeals as propaganda, as in his play *The Fall of British Tyranny*, were more suitable for a general audience about to face war. That the sixth chapter concludes with the notice "[To be continued.]" is perhaps a simple printer's error, Towne not having realized that Leacock intended to conclude the text with the sixth chapter. Perhaps printer Towne was already returning to the Tory side and no longer wished to print the patriot piece.[131]

The Text

The text that follows presents exact transcriptions of the first printings of each pamphlet chapter as printed by Benjamin Towne in Philadelphia. The Towne pamphlets are located at the New York Public Library. Although Towne published each chapter separately in pamphlet form, as shown in the table presented above, he numbered consecutively the pages of the pamphlet series. His page numbers are represented here in brackets in the text. Towne misnumbered in one place: he did not number any page 34. I omit catchword repetitions, although I insert the catchword silently in each of the few places that Towne did not repeat the word at the head of the following pamphlet page. I omit each chapter's concluding comments, such as "To be continued."

The following table may serve as a convenient reference:

Chapter	Pages	Philadelphia Printing	Evans Number
1	12	October 1774	13104
2	13–22	November 1774	13109
3	23–33	December 1774	13110
4	35–46	January 1775	13800
5	47–58	February 1775	13804
6	59–70	February 1775	13808

Notes to the Introduction

1. The section on Significance below more fully discusses the Puritan millennial vision, particularly with reference to the eighteenth century.

2. Moses Coit Tyler, *The Literary History of the American Revolution, 1763–1783*, 2 vols. (1897; reprint, New York: Barnes and Noble, 1941), 1:257, 258n.

3. M. Katherine Jackson, *Outlines of the Literary History of Colonial Pennsylvania* (Ph.D. diss., Columbia University, 1907; reprint, New York: AMS Press, 1966), 141.

4. George Everett Hastings, *The Life and Works of Francis Hopkinson* (Chicago: University of Chicago Press, 1926), 200, 199.

5. J. R. Bowman, "A Bibliography of *The First Book of the American Chronicles of the Times, 1774–1775*," *American Literature* 1 (1929): 69.

6. Arthur M. Schlesinger, *Prelude to Independence: The Newspaper War on Britain, 1764–1776* (New York: Alfred A. Knopf, 1958), 45.

7. Bruce I. Granger, *Political Satire in the American Revolution* (Ithaca: Cornell University Press, 1960), 70.

8. Bernard Bailyn, *The Ideological Origins of the American Revolution* (Cambridge: Harvard University Press, 1967), 10. The survey of commentary on *The First Book of the American Chronicles of the Times* omits mention of Philip Davidson, who quotes from the satire but makes no critical assessment whatsoever, in *Propaganda and the American*

Revolution, 1763–1783 (Chapel Hill: University of North Carolina Press, 1941), 212–13. Two more recent commentators on the appearance of Cromwell in the satire are James West Davidson and Alfred F. Young, whose works I use and comment on in the Significance section below. (See notes 101 and 114 below.)

9. Tyler, 1:257; Hastings, 199–200.

10. In 1980, I reproduced this broadside song and discussed its authorship in "John Leacock's *A New Song, On the Repeal of the Stamp-Act*," *Early American Literature* 15 (1980): 188–93.

11. Patricia H. Virga discussed the confusing evidence regarding authorship of *The Disappointment* and convincingly disputed the evidence naming Thomas Forrest as its author in *The American Opera to 1790* (Ann Arbor: UMI Research Press, 1982), 36–59. David Mays concluded, as Virga did, that Leacock did not write *The Disappointment*: David M. Mays, ed., *The Disappointment, or, the Force of Credulity* (Gainesville: University Press of Florida, 1976), 9–10, 36n.

12. John Fanning Watson, *Annals of Philadelphia, and Pennsylvania, in the Olden Time being a Collection of Memoirs, Anecdotes, and Incidents of the City and its Inhabitants, and of the Early Settlements of the Inland Part of Pennsylvania, from the days of the Founders* (Philadelphia: Published for the Author, 1850), 1:104; William Dunlap, *A History of the American Theatre* (New York: Harper, 1832), 409; James Rees, *The Dramatic Authors of America* (Philadelphia: G. B. Zieber, 1845), 98; Joseph Sabin, *Bibliotheca Americana: A Dictionary of Books Relating to America* (New York: Bibliographical Society of America, 1878), 10:141; Charles R. Hildeburn, *A Century of Printing: The Issues of the Press in Pennsylvania, 1685–1784* (Philadelphia: Matlack and Harvey, 1886), 2:249; George O. Seilhamer, *History of the American Theatre: During the Revolution and After* (Philadelphia: Globe Printing, 1889), 10; Paul Leicester Ford, *Some Notes towards an Essay on the Beginnings of American Dramatic Literature, 1606–1789* (New York: Printed for the Author, 1893), 20–21; Oscar Wegelin, *Early American Plays, 1714–1830* (New York: Dunlap Society, 1900), 54; Montrose J. Moses, *The American Dramatist* (Boston: Little, Brown, 1917), 291.

13. Francis James Dallett, Jr., "John Leacock and *The Fall of British Tyranny*," *The Pennsylvania Magazine of History and Biography* 78 (1954): 456–75.

14. It seems likely that Norman O. Philbrick simply did not know of Dallett's article when he wrote the editorial apparatus for the *The Fall of British Tyranny* in his anthology *Trumpets Sounding: Propaganda Plays of the American Revolution* (New York: Benjamin Blom, 1972).

15. Professor J. A. Leo Lemay informed me of this key advertisement.

16. My text for the play is that reproduced by Philbrick, 59–132. The quotation is from 4.7.

17. The two biblical references in the play that are not made in the satire are nonetheless drawn from the same Old Testament books from which nearly all the allusions in both works are taken. David is mentioned by name in the play (2.2; 4.6) but not in the satire. The story of Naaman, the leper, and the name Gehazi are both mentioned in the play but not in the satire.

18. For the most part, information in this discussion of Leacock's life can be found in the Dallett article and in the entry on Leacock in *Philadelphia: Three Centuries of American Art* (Philadelphia: Philadelphia Museum of Art, 1976), 70–72. Documents relating to Leacock and his relatives can be found in the American Philosophical Society, the Historical Society of Pennsylvania, and the Philadelphia City Hall records. A Cash-Leacock-White family genealogy is available in *The Papers of Benjamin Franklin*, ed. Leonard W. Labaree et al. (New Haven: Yale University Press, 1959–), 8:140–41.

Introduction 41

19. A picture of the whistle is featured in the article on Leacock in *Philadelphia: Three Centuries of American Art*. The whistle is part of a standing exhibition at the Philadelphia Museum of Art.

20. This very relevant point was first made by the author of the entry on Leacock in *Philadelphia: Three Centuries of American Art*.

21. Roy E. Goodman, Reference Librarian at the American Philosophical Society, has checked the membership register and informed me that Leacock was not a member of the Society. Leacock's entries in his commonplace book, located at the Society, show nonetheless that Leacock closely followed some of the Society's meetings, and he was particularly interested in farming experiments.

22. Patricia Virga first noted this information (316n.158), contained in the "Letters of John Leacock to John Cadwalader and James Logan" at the Historical Society of Pennsylvania.

23. Leacock asked Coombe to "present there in my behalf" his request that the Society promote local vine culture. Leacock to the American Philosophical Society, 29 December 1772.

24. The article in the *Pennsylvania Gazette* for 1 May 1765 (p. 1, cols. 1–2), for instance, might be Leacock's.

25. For general background on the social, economic, and intellectual impetuses for the Revolution, see Merrill Jensen, *The Founding of a Nation: The History of the American Revolution, 1763–1776* (New York: Oxford University Press, 1968); Gordon S. Wood, *The Creation of the American Republic, 1776–1787* (Chapel Hill: University of North Carolina Press for the Institute of Early American History and Culture, 1969); and H. Trevor Colbourn, *The Lamp of Experience: Whig History and the Intellectual Origins of the American Revolution* (1965; reprint, New York, W. W. Norton, 1974).

26. I discuss contemporary identification of the biblical characters in the Characters section below.

27. See the section on Printings and note 131 below.

28. Bailyn, *Ideological Origins*, 10.

29. See the section on Significance.

30. John Eliot, Robert Beverley, John Lawson, and Cadwallader Colden all early in the century had presented favorable views of the Indian. Colden's *History of the Five Indian Nations* (published in New York, 1727; expanded, 1747), for instance, insisted that the Indian possessed "heroic" qualities and portrayed the Indian community as close to an ideal republic. Drawing upon Locke's view of the original social contract and on enlightenment thought in general, Colden described the Indians as model republicans. Leacock plays upon this conception in a song written to honor Tammany, a legendary Indian chief, in his play, *The Fall of British Tyranny*. By the Revolution, Indians were not only accepted but had begun to be revered. See Richard Slotkin, *Regeneration Through Violence: The Mythology of the American Frontier, 1600–1860* (Middletown, Conn.: Wesleyan University Press, 1973), 199–201, and 313–68, esp. 329; J. A. Leo Lemay, "The Frontiersman from Lout to Hero: Notes on the Significance of the Comparative Method and the Stage Theory in Early American Literature and Culture," *American Antiquarian Society, Proceedings* 88 (1979): 199–211.

31. Brief biographies of the historical counterparts for characters appear below in the Notes to the Text section.

32. Schlesinger mistakenly quoted Tyler among his citations supposedly from the *American Chronicles*. He evidently agreed with Tyler, however, about the identification of Jeremiah as Samuel Adams. See *Prelude*, 45.

33. Granger, 69.

34. Clifford K. Shipton, *Sibley's Harvard Graduates: Biographical Sketches of Those Who attended Harvard College*, vols. 4–16 (Cambridge: Harvard University Press and Massachusetts Historical Society, 1932–1972), 11:198.

35. An entry on Cooper appears in William F. Sprague, *Annals of the American Pulpit*, 12 vols. (New York: Robert Carter and Brothers, 1857), 1:442. Shipton, of course, also wrote on Cooper, *Sibley's*, 11:199ff. Frederick Tuckerman prepared two brief editions of Cooper's personal papers, "The Diary of Samuel Cooper, 1775–1776," *American Historical Review* 6 (1901): 301–41, and "Letters of Samuel Cooper to Thomas Pownall, 1769–1777," *American Historical Review* 8 (1903): 301–30. Another early discussion of Cooper is in Alice M. Baldwin, *The New England Clergy and the American Revolution* (Durham: Duke University Press, 1928). Charles Akers followed his three articles about Cooper with the first full-length biography of the pastor of the Brattle Street Church, *The Divine Politician: Samuel Cooper and the American Revolution* (Boston: Northeastern University Press, 1982). In *Religion and the American Mind* (Cambridge: Harvard University Press, 1966), Alan Heimert remarked, "Of the Congregational clergy of the metropolis only Samuel Cooper and, to a degree, Chauncy were at all active in these years in the service of Whig patriotism" (418). But Akers disagreed: "[W]ith few exceptions Boston's Congregational clergy sincerely preached the Whig political ideology in the religious idiom that for the majority of Americans remained meaningful and reinforcing of the personal, social, and economic forces behind resistance" (182).

36. Akers, 117.

37. Akers makes this connection early in his biography of Cooper (2). Cooper was undoubtedly aware of the economic consequences for his merchant congregation if resistance to the Crown were actively pursued; Boston's elite, many of them merchants, attended Cooper's Brattle Street Church (Akers, 2, 26, 175).

38. Shipton, *Sibley's*, 11:199.

39. Stephen E. Patterson believes Cooper is the clergyman Hutchinson most feared; see *Political Parties in Revolutionary Massachusetts* (Madison: University of Wisconsin Press, 1973), 88.

40. See Shipton, *Sibley's*, 11:199. The letters were sent to Thomas Cushing.

41. See Shipton, *Sibley's*, 11:199.

42. Some of the letters appear among the Franklin *Papers* 20:110–15, 232–35, 480–82, 499–505; 21:273–76, 297–302.

43. Quoted in Sprague, *Annals*, 1:441.

Ephraim Eliot's commonplace book contains another laudatory comment about Cooper's preaching:

> In Brattle Street men were charmed into the ways of wisdom by the eloquent, the graceful Doctor Samuel Cooper. With a voice melodious in the tones of a delicate flute, with an elegant address, in Attic diction, he allured his hearers to virtue, with a soothing tenderness he poured the oil and the wine into the wounded bosom, and in persuasive language he recalled the vicious from the paths which lead to Death.

Quoted in Shipton, *Sibley's*, 11:194.

44. Quoted in Shipton, *Sibley's*, 11:194. The comment appeared in Belcher's letter-book for 12 September 1750.

45. See Akers, 182.

46. John Adams, *Diary and Autobiography of John Adams*, ed. L. H. Butterfield, 4 vols. (Cambridge: Harvard University Press, 1961–66), 2:81.

47. Samuel Cooper, *A Sermon Preached before his Excellency Thomas Pownall, Esq . . . October 16th, 1759. Upon Occasion of the Success of His Majesty's Arms in the Reduction of Quebec* (Boston, [1759]), 48.

48. Hatch explains the mechanism by which the clergy adapted Whig ideology into a religious idiom in *The Sacred Cause of Liberty: Republican Thought and the Millennium in Revolutionary New England* (New Haven: Yale University Press, 1977), 46–47.

49. Shipton, *Sibley's*, 11:197, reports the Cooper epithet. In his introduction to *The Geneva Bible: A Facsimile of the 1560 Edition* (Madison: University of Wisconsin Press, 1969), Lloyd E. Berry points out that one of the most famous of Elizabethan preachers—who, as a group, generally used the Geneva Bible—Henry Smith, was called "silver tongued Smith" for his eloquence. Leacock used the Geneva Bible for the biblical texts he appropriated. See the comments immediately following the text.

50. *The Boston Ministers: A Ballad*, written about 1774, circulated in manuscript for many years, developing variants as it circulated. This version is from *The New England Historical and Genealogical Register*, 1859.

51. Bolton delivered his "oration" at a mock town meeting of royal officers. Akers points out that it was probably published first in New York, "for no Boston printer, despite the presence of the army, would have dared so to provoke the Sons of Liberty" (193). The quotation here is from the Boston printing of the Bolton *Oration*, 1775 (Evans no. 13840), 8.

52. Peter Oliver, *Peter Oliver's Origin and Progress of the American Rebellion: A Tory View* [1781], ed. Douglass Adair and John A. Schutz (San Marino, Calif.: Huntington Library, 1963), 43, 44–45. Oliver later on in the volume referred to "the serpentine *Dr. Cooper*" who "committed such atrocious Acts as will perpetuate his Name with indelible Infamy" (74). This, from a man who began his "history" by assuring his readers that he would report only the truth, without exaggeration: "I promise You I will adhere most sacredly to Truth, & endeavor to steer as clear as possible from Exaggeration" (9).

53. See Akers, 188–89.

54. See Akers, 168.

55. See Akers, 193.

56. See Patterson, 76–77; Shipton, *Sibley's*, 11:197.

57. John Andrews, *The Letters of John Andrews, Esq., of Boston, 1772–1776*, ed. Winthrop Sargent (Cambridge: John Wilson and Sons, 1866), 17.

58. See Akers, 188.

59. Quoted in Baldwin, 94.

60. Shipton, *Sibley's*, 6:442.

Slotkin has pointed out that Chauncy's *Letter to a Friend*, on Braddock's defeat and the American Sir William Johnson's victory at Lake George, "echoes the phraseology of Matherian attacks on Puritan complacency in his suggestion that the chief use of the defeat is its terminating our sense of 'security'" (228). In *Old Brick: Charles Chauncy of Boston, 1705–1787* (Minneapolis: University of Minnesota Press, 1980), Chauncy's biographer Edward Griffin speaks of the jeremiad theme in Chauncy's sermons, stating that Chauncy "not only bewailed the spiritual sluggishness of the times and the danger of Anglican inroads, he also insisted on the obligation of young people . . . to revive and continue the noble heritage of their forebears" (31).

61. Shipton, *Sibley's*, 6:442.

62. Heimert has discussed this aspect of Chauncy's theology (284). Heimert asserted that the jeremiad sermon form reflected a "belief that all difficulties came as punishments for a society's sins, that these afflictions could be removed only by repentance, and that their removal was occasion for demonstration that such repentance had been sincere" (284).

63. See Charles Chauncy, *A Discourse on "the good News from a far Country." Delivered July 24th. A Day of Thanks-giving . . . on Occasion of the Repeal of the Stamp Act*, in John Wingate Thornton, *The Pulpit of the American Revolution* (Boston: Gould and Lincoln, 1860), 143–44.

64. Hatch, 53.
65. See Hatch, 53–54.
66. The letter appears in the Franklin *Papers*, 21:347.
67. See note 50.
68. Patterson has remarked that Hancock's "actions in the early 1770s reveal a shrewdness that should not be underestimated," 72.
69. See the Franklin *Papers*, 20:123, 237–38. John Adams's diary entry for Saturday, 24 April 1774, attests to Hancock's response to the letters: "Mr. Hancock is deeply affected, is determined in conjunction with Majr. Hawley to watch the vile Serpent, and his deputy Serpent Brattle" (2:81).
70. John Hancock, *An Oration delivered March 5, 1774* (Boston, 1774), 18.
71. Akers, 171. Akers has discussed the *Oration* and the controversy over its authorship (168–72).
72. Shipton, *Sibley's*, 13:429–30.
73. *The Dictionary of American English on Historical Principles*, ed. William A. Craigie and James Hulbert, 4 vols. (Chicago: University of Chicago Press, 1942), reports that J. R. Shaw in his *Life* (1807) wrote of his having been introduced "to a fine parcel of ladies [prostitutes] (all Mother Carey's chickens)." This *Dictionary* is hereafter cited as *DAE*.
74. Mark Mayo Boatner III in his *Encyclopedia of the American Revolution* (New York: David McKay, 1966) points out that by 1788, legends of Putnam's heroism had become so abundant that David Humphreys capitalized on the interest in Putnam and wrote a "biography." In his *Life of Putnam* (1788), Humphreys created a larger-than-life American hero. The biography, *An Essay on the Life of the Honourable Major-General Israel Putnam* is conveniently reprinted in William Bottorff, ed., *The Miscellaneous Works of David Humphreys* (1804; reprint Gainesville, Fla.: Scholars' Facsimiles and Reprints, 1968).
75. See Jensen, 492, 535–37.
76. Horace Walpole's letter with the biblical parodic satire is printed in *Horace Walpole's Correspondence with Sir Horace Mann*, vol. 1 [of four], as vol. 17 of *The Yale Edition of Horace Walpole's Correspondence*, ed. W. S. Lewis et al. (New Haven: Yale University Press, 1954), 491–97. Albert C. Matthews makes the same point in "The Book of America," *Massachusetts Historical Society, Proceedings* 62 (1930): 171–97.
77. *Walpole's Correspondence*, 1 [17]:491n.
78. Colbourn, 19.
79. The *Chronicle of the Kings of England* was printed again in Boston in 1759 and saw two other American editions in the early 1770s. Robert Bell, in association with Benjamin Towne (Leacock's printer), brought out the last edition in 1774; see Colbourn, 19–20.
80. I have found no critical commentary on this satire.
81. See Edward Field, ed., *The State of Rhode Island and Providence Plantations at the End of the Century*, 2 vols. (Boston: Mason Publishing, 1902), 1:209–19; Davidson, 11; and Bailyn, 10.
82. See Albert C. Matthews, "The Book of America," *Massachusetts Historical Society, Proceedings* 62 (1930): 171–97. "The Book of America" is mentioned by Davidson (243) and by Granger (34–35, 70n.). For "The Book of Harvard" see William C. Lane, "The Rebellion of 1766 in Harvard College," *Colonial Society of Massachusetts, Publications* (1905): 33–59. Parodic biblical satires mocking aspects of college life were popular forms of entertainment for the students. Joel Barlow joined the tradition in January 1777, when he satirized the ineffectual Yale President Naphtali Daggett. The satire was evidently first printed by Anson Phelps Stokes, in *Memorials of Eminent Yale Men*, 2 vols. (New Haven: Yale University Press, 1914), 1:127; it was reprinted by James

Woodress, *A Yankee's Odyssey: The Life of Joel Barlow* (1958; reprint, New York: Greenwood Press, 1968), 44–45.

83. See Samuel Oppenheim, "The Chapters of Isaac the Scribe: A Bibliographic Rarity, New York, 1772," *Publications of the American Jewish Historical Society* 22 (1914): 39–51.

84. These hoaxes appear, with a discussion of their provenance and printings, in the Franklin *Papers*, 6:114–28. For Leacock's family relationship to Deborah Read, see the *Papers*, 8:140–41.

85. "A Prophecy" is printed in Francis Hopkinson, *The Miscellaneous Essays and Occasional Writings of Francis Hopkinson*, 3 vols. (Philadelphia: T. Dobson, 1792), 1:92–97. It is discussed by Granger, 236–37.

86. The complete 1775 pamphlet title evidently was *Some Chapters of the Book of Chronicles of Isaac the Scribe, Written on his Passage from the Land of the Amerikites to the Island of the Albionites;* Evans evidently could find no copy of the pamphlet to reproduce. *Isaac the Scribe* is mentioned by Davidson, 212–13, and its newspaper and pamphlet versions are discussed by Samuel Oppenheim (see note 83).

87. I have found no critical commentary on Nuel Bostwick's satire.

88. *A Ministerial Catechise* is briefly discussed by Bailyn, 10, 15; and Davidson, 212.

89. Bailyn mentions *Some Strictures* (121, 127).

90. Bible parody has perhaps been around as long as the Bible has. That the biblical texts become re-constituted as new, parodic texts does not necessarily indicate that those biblical texts are being satirized in the new texts. In *A Theory of Parody: The Teachings of Twentieth-Century Art Forms* (New York: Methuen, 1985), Linda Hutcheon suggests that the re-constitution of a text into a new, parodic text might not signal an effect of ridicule for the text parodied (6, 10, 37–38, and passim). I treat the parodic implications of *The First Book of the American Chronicles of the Times* below.

91. A vast amount of research has been done in this field. Most of my comments below on typology and millennialism in England are based on Katharine R. Firth, *The Apocalyptic Tradition in Reformation Britain, 1530–1645* (Oxford: Oxford University Press, 1979); Paul J. Korshin, *Typologies in England, 1650-1820* (Princeton: Princeton University Press, 1982): Bernard Capp, "The Political Dimension of Apocalyptic Thought," C. A. Patrides, "'Something like Prophetick strain': Apocalyptic Configurations in Milton," and Paul J. Korshin, "Queuing and Waiting: The Apocalypse in England, 1660–1750," in *The Apocalypse in English Renaissance Thought and Literature: Patterns, Antecedents, and Repercussions*, ed. C. A. Patrides and Joseph Wittreich (Manchester: Manchester University Press, 1984), 93–124, 207–37, and 240–65; J. F. C. Harrison, *The Second Coming: Popular Millenarianism, 1780–1850* (London: Routledge and Kegan Paul, 1979); and Clarke Garrett, *Respectable Folly: Millenarians and the French Revolution in France and England* (Baltimore: Johns Hopkins University Press, 1975).

92. See Firth, 1–31.

93. The fear of Roman Catholic domination was perhaps most prominent, but Katharine Firth has pointed out that in addition to the threat of the papacy, the threat of Turkish invasion dominated much of the apocalyptic and millennial writings: "The presence of the Turkish threat to the Empire also heightened expectation of the end of the world. In the 1530s [especially] . . . the immediacy of the world's end formed a central theme of writings in the apocalyptic tradition" (19).

Millenarians were obsessed with numbers, dates, and times, some asserting that Christ had already come, some that Christ's arrival was imminent. See Firth, 15–31, and passim.

94. See Korshin, *Typologies*, 3–39.

95. Korshin, "Queuing," 241.
96. Korshin, "Queuing," 241.
97. Sacvan Bercovitch gives this interpretation a full treatment in *The Puritan Origins of the American Self* (New Haven: Yale University Press, 1975) and *The American Jeremiad* (Madison: University of Wisconsin Press, 1978). Melvin B. Endy, Jr., takes issue with Bercovitch's interpretation with regard to the American Revolution in "Just War, Holy War, and Millennialism in Revolutionary America," *William and Mary Quarterly*, 3d ser., 42 (1985): 3–25. One cannot test the validity of Endy's views, for his argument lacks concrete examples by way of evidence to support his broad assertions.

In *The Faithful Shepherd: A History of the New England Ministry in the Seventeenth Century* (Chapel Hill: University of North Carolina Press for the Institute of Early American History and Culture, 1972), David D. Hall discusses the apocalyptic speculations of the leading ministers of New England (227–48). A very brief survey of the ministers who used apocalyptic imagery in their sermons is available in Stephen J. Stein, "Transatlantic Extensions: Apocalyptic in Early New England," in *The Apocalypse in English Renaissance Thought and Literature*, ed. C. A. Patrides and Joseph Wittreich (Manchester: Manchester University Press, 1984), 266–98.

98. See Bercovitch, *Puritan Origins*, 98, 100.
99. Cromwell was thus conceived as both merciful and militant. For commentary on Marvell's figuring of Cromwell in the *First Anniversary*, see Korshin, *Typologies*, 68–70, and "Queuing," 250–52.

100. See Korshin, *Typologies*, 69. Christopher Hill discusses popular conceptions of Cromwell and their relations to millennialism in *God's Englishman: Oliver Cromwell and the English Revolution* (New York: Dial Press, 1970), 253–76, and passim; *Antichrist in Seventeenth-Century England* (London: Oxford University Press, 1971); and *The World Turned Upside Down: Radical Ideas during the English Revolution* (New York: Viking Press, 1972), 70–85 and passim.

It should be noted that I am presenting the Puritan point of view here; royalists saw the restoration of monarchy to Charles II as their own signification of Christ's second coming. See Capp, 117–18; Korshin, "Queuing," 251–52.

101. In *The Puritan Experiment: New England Society from Bradford to Edwards* (New York: St. Martin's Press, 1976), Francis J. Bremer notes that the New England Puritans' support for the English Revolution was so widespread that in 1644 alone, the Massachusetts Bay Puritans held twelve special fast days; in addition, Bremer attests, many New Englanders held eminent posts in the Parliamentary Army (108–12). According to one study, nearly half of the highly trained ministers and university men returned to support Cromwell's cause; see Harry Stout, "The Morphology of Remigration: New England University Men and their Return to England, 1640–1660," *Journal of American Studies* 10 (1976): 151–72.

In my discussion of the New England opinion about Cromwell in the seventeenth and eighteenth centuries, I have found indispensible the excellent essay by Alfred F. Young, "English Plebeian Culture and Eighteenth-Century Radicalism," in *The Origins of Anglo-American Radicalism*, ed. Margaret Jacob and James Jacob (London: Allen and Unwin, 1984), 185–212.

102. Young, 194.
103. Young, 195, 197–98.
104. Young, 195–200.
105. Young has pointed out that "[C]ommon American experience suggests a few fairly good indicators of the memory of an individual becoming the property of large masses of people: when he is known by his first name alone . . .; when parents name their children after him; or when places lay claim to his presence" (197).

106. Ludlow, a regicide, became one of Cromwell's bitterest critics. His memoirs, published in 1698–99, steadily pointed to Cromwell's tyranny, to effect Ludlow's hope that "men may learn from the issue of Cromwellian tyranny, that liberty and a standing mercenary army are incompatible" (quoted and discussed in Colbourn, 44). Colbourn notes that Jefferson owned the 1698–99 edition of Ludlow (44). See also Young, 195.

107. Colbourn quotes and discusses the influence of Catherine Macaulay (43–45). See also Young, 195; and Lucy M. Donnelly, "The Celebrated Mrs. Macaulay," *William and Mary Quarterly*, 3d ser., 6 (1949): 191, 193–94, 202. In *The Enlightenment in America* (Oxford: Oxford University Press, 1976), Henry F. May comments on the relative popularity of David Hume's *History of England* and Macaulay's work, 119, 157, and passim.

108. Quoted by Colbourn, 79.

109. Adams, *Diary*, 1:220.

110. Young, 195.

111. Young, 195.

112. Young discusses this aspect of revolutionary propaganda (199).

113. Alan Heimert is perhaps the first in a long line of historians who have shown the relevance of the Great Awakening to the rise of revolutionary agitation. Melvin B. Endy, Jr., surveys and comments on several of these interpretations. Jon Butler's essay, "The Future of American Religious History: Prospectus, Agenda, Transatlantic *Problematique*," *William and Mary Quarterly*, 3d ser., 42 (1985): 167–83 commends more recent interpretations.

114. Quoted and discussed by James West Davidson, *The Logic of Millennial Thought: Eighteenth-Century New England* (New Haven: Yale University Press, 1977), 17, and passim.

115. James West Davidson, 29, and passim.

116. James West Davidson discusses the enthusiasts' conceptions of the significance of earthquakes in the eighteenth century (95–121).

117. Alfred Young has argued that the existence of Cromwell as a kind of *deux ex machina* (my words) in *The First Book of the American Chronicles of the Times* is explainable solely because of the non-elite attitudes toward Cromwell. While Young finds humor, he evidently finds no ironic or satiric effect from Cromwell's appearance. I agree that the satire was most likely popular with the non-elite audience, as Young has shown; for reasons having to do with the form of the satire, I argue that the satire offers as much for the elite as for the non-elite culture.

James West Davidson notes that one effect of the depiction of Cromwell is criticism of his hypocrisy, but Davidson makes no further comment on the text as a whole (239–40).

118. See Hutcheon's *Theory of Parody*, 69–83. Hutcheon's theoretical models, derived from study of art forms, seem to me very appropriate to the study of eighteenth-century parody. In *Parody//Metafiction: An Analysis of Parody as a Critical Mirror to the Writing and Reception of Fiction* (London: Croom Helm, 1979), Margaret A. Rose discusses the formal effects of parodic self-reference.

119. Samuel Johnson, *A Dictionary of the English Language*, 2 vols. (London: W. Strahan, 1755), s.v. "parody."

120. I have condensed Hutcheon's dense discussion of the paradox of parody, 69–79.

121. Samuel Johnson's 1755 definition of parody tells us as much. For twentieth-century verification, see Hutcheon, 5–6, 32, and passim.

122. See Hutcheon, 5–6, 31–35, for clarification of the definition. Hutcheon discusses Mikhail Bakhtin's theory of double-directed discourse and the carnivalesque, 69–75.

123. Hutcheon, 62.

124. Hutcheon, 62.

125. See Young, 198.

126. The plebeian culture in England emigrated in large masses during the eighteenth century. Many of the common people in Massachusetts and elsewhere probably saw during their lifetimes at least one mummer demonstration featuring Cromwell. See Young, 196.

127. Peter Karsten, *Patriot Heroes in England and America: Political Symbolism and Changing Values over Three Centuries* (Madison, Wis.: University of Wisconsin Press, 1979), 7.

128. Hutcheon, 19.

129. See Hutcheon, 3–5.

130. Under item 11 in his bibliography of the printings of the *American Chronicles*, Bowman mistakenly noted that the second chapter had been advertised in the *Pennsylvania Packet* twice, once on 14 November and once on 21 November 1774. But the *Pennsylvania Packet* advertisement of 14 November is for chapter 1, not chapter 2.

Thomas R. Adams does not list *The First Book of the American Chronicles of the Times*.

131. Towne's political activities are discussed by Dwight L. Teeter in "Benjamin Towne: The Precarious Career of a Persistent Printer," *The Pennsylvania Magazine of History and Biography* 89 (1965): 316–30.

JOHN LEACOCK'S

*The First Book
of the American Chronicles
of the Times,
1774–1775*

The First Book of the American Chronicles of the Times

The first Book of the American Chronicles of the Times.

CHAP. I.

AND behold! when the tidings came to the great city that is afar off,[1] the city that is in the land of Britain, how the men of Boston, even the Bostonites, had arose, a great multitude, and destroyed the TEA, the abominable merchandize of the east,[2] and cast it into the midst of the sea.

2. That the Lord the King waxed exceeding wroth,[3] insomuch that the form of his visage was changed,[4] and his knees smote one against the other.

3. Then he assembled together the Princes, the Nobles, the Counsellors, the Judges, and all the Rulers of the people, even the great Sanhedrim,[5] and when he had told them what things were come to pass,

4. They smote their breasts and said, These men fear thee not, O King, neither have they obeyed the voice of our Lord the King, nor worshipped the TEA CHEST, which thou hast set up, whose length was three cubits, and the breadth thereof one cubit and an half.

[2] 5. Now therefore make a decree[6] that their harbours be blocked up, and their ports shut, that their merchants may be broke, and their multitudes perish, that there may be no more the voice of merchandize heard in the land, that their ships, that goeth upon the waters, may be sunk in the depths thereof, and their mariners dwindle away to nought, that their cods and their oil may stink, and the whale, the great Leviathan, may be no more troubled, for that they have rebelled against thee.

6. And it came to pass that the King hearkened unto the voice, unto the voice of these sons of Belial.[7]

7. Then arose Mordecai, the Benjamite, who was fourscore and five years old, an aged man whom the Lord loved, a wise man, a soothsayer, an astrologer, in whom was wisdom from above,[8] and he said unto the King, I pray thee, O King, let thy servant speak,

8. And the King commanded that he should speak.

9. Then Mordecai spake aloud, in the presence of all the Princes, the Nobles, the Counsellors, the Judges, and all the Rulers of the people, and said, O King, live for ever.[9]

10. Thy throne, O King, is encompassed about with lies, and thy servants, the Bernardites[10] and the Hutchinsonians,[11] are full of deceit, for be it known unto thee, O King, they hide the truth from thee, and wrongfully accuse the men of Boston, for behold, these [3] letters in mine hand[12] witnesseth sore against them, O King, if thou art wise, thou wilt understand these things.

11. And there was present one of the King's Counsellors, a Jacobite, a vagabond, a Wedderburnite,[13] and he used foul language, and said unto Mordecai, Thou liest; and Mordecai answered, and said unto him, God will smite thee, thou whited wall, and Mordecai departed from amongst them.[14]

12. And behold the Princes, the Nobles, the Counsellors, the Judges, and all the Rulers of the people, cried out vehemently against Mordecai,[15] for they were in fear because of Mordecai's wisdom.

13. And they besought the King that he would take from Mordecai his post,[16] for he was in high honour before that time.

14. So they prevailed on the King, and he took from Mordecai his post, and all that he had, and Mordecai was persecuted yet more and more,[17] but he bore it patiently, for Job[18] was his grandfather's great grandfather; moreover, he knew the times must alter, and the King's eyes would be opened anon.

15. Now in the Seventh Month, in the fourteenth day of the month, the Lord the King commanded Thomas, the Captain of the Gageites,[19] saying,

16. Choose thou the valiant men of Britain, by hundreds and by thousands, and get ye together the ships, even the ships of war, the [4] terror of the nations round about, and make your way towards the coasts of the Americanites, the land of the Bostonites,[20] that lieth on the other side the great sea westwards, and cut off all that pisseth against the wall, and utterly destroy all their cities with fire and with sword, for they have rebelled against me.

17. Howbeit, the men of Boston had intelligence thereof, for they kept their spies abroad,[21] from the east to the west and from the north to the south; and when the tidings came of these things, they rent their clothes, and fasted, put on sackcloth, and went softly.[22]

18.[23] And the Bostonites, the men of New-England, spake unto Jedediah the scribe,[24] that he would bring the book of the law[25] of their fathers, which the Lord had commanded they should obey.

19. Then Jedediah, the priest, brought the book of the law before the congregation, both of men and women that could understand it.

20. And he read therein, in the street that was before the Water-gate, and in the Market-place, and at the entry of the Fish-gate, and in the Old South, from the morning until the midday, and from the midday until the evening.[26]

21. For Jedediah the priest had understanding of the times to know what the Americanites ought to do, and what they ought [5] not to do, and all his brethren were at his commandment.[27]

22. And the ears of all the people hearkened unto the book of the law,[28] and

entered into a solemn league and covenant,[29] that they would obey the book of the law, and none other, both the priests and the Levites.

23. And behold, when Thomas, the Gageite, was come into the land of the Bostonites, he threatened them sore, and swore by the life of Pharoah, insomuch that some of the old women and children lifted up their voices, and wept exceedingly with bitter lamentations.

24. And it came to pass that the New-Yorkites, the Philadelphites, the Marylandites, the Virginites, the Carolinites, took pity on their brethren the Bostonites, for there was like to be a famine in the land.[30]

25. And they got ready their camels and their asses, their mules and their oxen, and laded them with their meat, their fine wheaten flour, their rice, their corn, their beeves and their sheep, and their figs and their raisins, and their wine and their oil, and their tobacco abundantly, and six thousand shekels of silver, and threescore talents of gold, and sent them, by the hands of the Levites, to their brethren, and there was joy in the land.[31]

26. Now this same Thomas, a Heathen, put forth a mock proclamation for the encouragement of piety,[32]

[6] 27. Then Jedediah the priest, and Obadiah,[33] and Ezekiel,[34] and Jonathan the son of Ebenezer,[35] stood up and said, Men and brethren (the Lord knoweth our hearts, and that we fear the Lord) ye have seen how this Heathen maketh a mock of holy things, and profaneth the GOD of our fathers, this man is like unto a Pharisee, he prayeth with his windows open, and a two edged sword at our throats. Moreover, he defileth the sabbath, in that he traineth his men on the Lord's day,[36] and have ye not seen with your eyes how he stoppeth the way side, that the congregation may not pass, and how that he putteth the yoke of cannon upon the neck of the Bostonites, and the people marvelled and said, Fye upon thee, Thomas! fye upon thee, Thomas! the Lord will avenge himself of such abominations.

28. Now be of good comfort, let us send messengers into all the coasts of our brethren, the Americanites, peradventure they will commune with us,[37] for we be one people, and serve one GOD: If so be they hear us, the Lord is on our side; but if they refuse to hearken to us, they and we be slaves to the Gageites, and our substance and all that we have taken from us, and we be their hewers of wood and drawers of water.[38]

29. And all the people shouted, and said with one voice, Send and commune with our brethren.[39]

[7] 30. Now it came to pass that their brethren listened unto them, and they sent messengers backwards and forwards throughout the land, from the east unto the west, and from the north unto the south, even unto the sea coast of the Georgeites.

31. And they assembled themselves together, in a congress in the great city of Philadelphia, in the house of the carpenters, the builders house, in the land of

Pennsylvania, on the seventh day of the Ninth Month,[40] with their coaches, their chariots, their camels, their horsemen, and their servants, a great multitude, and they communed together.

32.[41] And behold, while they thus communed, certain Torykites, false prophets and friends to the Gageites, said, Let us distract their counsels, and set at nought their congress, we will cause a lying spirit to go throughout their land, that the great city of the Bostonites is burned to the ground, and the inhabitants thereof are slain by the edge of the sword, peradventure they will return home to inquire after their wives, their little ones, and their sheep and their oxen, and we be then rewarded by our Lord the King.

33. And the rumour thereof spread abroad throughout all the land, and messengers were sent day by day.

34. And moreover, that Thomas the Gageite, the Captain of the Heathen, came by night and stole away their powder and their [8] implements for war, and to seize their brethren and send them away captives to Babel, to be tried by the Heathen laws,[42] and peradventure hanged for their supposed transgressions.

35. Then arose Jedediah the priest, and Aminadab,[43] and Obadiah, and Jeremiah,[44] and lifted up their voices, and spake aloud and said,

36. Fathers, brethren, and the children of our fathers, ye have heard of all the evil that has been brought upon our city, the city of our forefathers, the New Canaan,[45] the land of promise, and behold this day it is desolate and no man dwelleth therein.

37. How doth the city remain solitary that was full of people; she is as a widow:[46] She that was great amongst the nations, and princess among the provinces, is about to be made tributary, and bow down to the TEA CHEST, the God of the Heathen; tell it not in Gath, nor publish it in the streets of Askalon.[47]

38. Now, therefore, if it seemeth good unto you, and that it proceedeth of the Lord our GOD, we will send to and fro unto our brethren that are in all the land of the Americanites (for with them are Priests and Levites in the cities and suburbs thereof) that they may assemble themselves unto us.[48]

39. And all the congregation answered and said, Let us do so, for the thing seemeth good [9] in the eyes of all the people,[49] for surely they will not be like the Gibeonites of old.

40. And they yet spake unto them and said, Now, therefore, we pray ye arise![50] Every man of you from sixteen to sixty get up, be strong and valiant, gird thy sword upon thy thigh, O thou most mighty, are ye not the men, and are ye not the sons of your fathers, that subdued the Louisburgites?[51]

41. And the young men gave a great shout and said, Yea, verily, we have heard with our ears, and our fathers have declared unto us, the noble deeds which they did in your days, and in the old time before us.

42. And Jedediah the priest, and Aminadab, and Obadiah, yet spake once more to the people and said, Moreover, brethren, are ye not valiant men, and

sprang from the tribe of the Oliverians, be not afraid, nor dismayed,[52] the Lord is on our side, we fight the battles of the Lord,[53] let us drive the Heathen out of our land, for they are but as grasshoppers unto us, and all the congregation gave a mighty shout and said, Lead us on; and Caleb[54] and his brethren, ten men in number, were sent as spies.

43. And they caused messengers to go throughout all the land, from Farmingham to Salem, and from Salem to Seabrook, and from Seabrook to Plymouth, and from Plymouth to Nantucket, and from Nantucket to Marblehead, and from Marblehead through Connecticut, and from Connecticut through[10]out all the cities, and along the sea coasts, and the borders thereof, and the valiant men assembled themselves, and marched to the relief of the men of Boston.

44. The Captains of hundreds, and the Captains of thousands,[55] and all the people, from the least even to the greatest, came to fight the battles of the Lord.

45. And the tribes of the valiant men from the mountains and from the country afar back, and as thou goest down to the sea coast, and they pitched their tents, which were of the skins of lions, and of bears, and of wolves, and of foxes, and of he-goats, and encamped in the valley of Ephraim.[56]

46.[57] And these are the names of the tribes, and the number of them that were sealed (that is, that had sworn by the solemn league and covenant) the least of whom could resist an hundred, and the greatest a thousand, valiant men of war, and apt for battle, which could handle a spear and shield, and their faces were like the faces of lions, and whose feet were like the roes in the mountains in swiftness.[58]

47. Of the tribe of Aminadab and Jedediah the priest, that were sealed, which were reckoned by their genealogies seventeen thousand and seven hundred and ninety and two, whose staves were like unto white oak saplins.

48. Of the tribe of Obadiah that were sealed, six thousand and four hundred and seventy and two, and their sons, and their sons sons, that could handle the strong bow and javelin.

[11] 49. Of the tribe of Ezekiel that were sealed, four thousand and four hundred and sixty and six, whose fists were as the hoofs of an elephant, and could beat down the Colossus at Rhodes.[59]

50. Of the tribe of Israel[60] and Jonathan[61] the sons of Ebenezer, that were sealed, ten thousand and six hundred and forty and nine that could sling a stone to a hair's breadth.[62]

51. Of the tribe of Nathan,[63] and Eleazer,[64] and Reuben,[65] and Hezekiah,[66] and Caleb, which were sealed, forty thousand and three hundred and fourscore and nineteen, five heads of the houshold of their fathers, all chosen men, and men of valour from their youth, exceeding Goliah of Gath[67] in height.

52. Of the tribe of Pelatiah[68] and Zedekiah,[69] which were sealed, five thousand and six hundred fourscore and one, the least of whom were stronger than Sampson,[70] bold men, and as hard as a pine knot.[71]

53. Of the tribe of Zechariah,[72] the sons of Joshua,[73] which were sealed, twenty thousand and three hundred thirty and one, men of high renown, which have done mighty feats.

54. Now these are the names and the numbers of their tribes.

55. Now it came to pass that when the Gageites beheld them afar off on their way, even as the sand on the sea shore in number, with their slings, and their darts, and their cross bows, and their spears, and their javelins in their hands, that they were astonied,[74] and [12] fear came upon them, and they said one to another, Let us flee to our own country afar off, for these be not men but unconquerable devils.

56. Howbeit, while the Gageites were about to flee,[75] the spies returned and spake to the Bostonites, as they were on their way (for each man marched a step with a gigantic stride of three cubits and a half, and a span) and said, Behold, brethren, your city, the city of our forefathers, even the city of our GOD, is safe, and your brethren, your wives, and your little ones, your cattle and your sheep are all in health, for the Heathen have not destroyed them.

57. So the rumour ceased, and the people gave a shout, a mighty shout, which was heard even in the camp of the Heathen afar off, and they said who did dare to spread this rumour, behold! are there not tar and feathers enow in our Land for these disturbers of our quiet.

58. And the men departed every man to his own home in peace, and the priests returned and blessed the Lord.

59. Now the rest of the acts of the Gageites, and all that they did, first and last, and all their abominations, behold will they not be written in the book of the Lamentations of the Elders and Select Men of Boston.

CHAP. II.

Now after these things, behold Thomas, sirnamed the Gageite, wrote letters unto the King, and sent them by the hands of Judas the parasite,[1] saying,

2.[2] The land thou sent us to subdue, is a land that eateth up thy people, for the men we saw in it are mightier in understanding than we.

3. Moreover they be giants, men of great stature, and we seemed but as caterpillars in their sight, they assemble in such multitudes, and come on so fast that they seem minded to do us mischief, so maliciously are their hearts set against us.

4. They hold altogether, and keep themselves close, and mark our steps, while they seem to lay wait for us, they roar in the midst of themselves, and set up their banners for tokens.[3]

5. O King, thy servant is in a great strait, the men of New England are stiffnecked[4] and [14] as stubborn hogs, neither knoweth thy servant what to make of them; they are worse unto me than all the plagues of Egypt.[5]

6. For they resolve upon resolves, they address, they complain, they protest, they compliment, they flatter, they sooth, and they threaten to root me up.

7. Now therefore, O King, I pray thee send able counsellors over, that they may advise and counsel thy servant, lest they circumvent him and he appear foolish in the eyes of all the people, for thou knowest, O King, thy servant is no conjuror.

8. Moreover, all my counsellors have forsaken me and resigned,[6] and are become like unto Job's comforters,[7] thy servant knoweth not what to do.

9. For the men of New England are as venomous as the poison of a serpent, even like the deaf adder that stoppeth her ears,[8] they give good words with their mouths, but curse with their hearts, they go too and fro in the evening, and grin like a dog, and run about through the city, they slander thy servant, they make a bye-word[9] of him, and grudge him every thing, yet complain if they be not satisfied.

10. Surely, O King, the spirit of Oliver or the Devil[10] is got in them.

11. Now behold, in process of time Rehoboam, the King,[11] sent messengers unto Thomas the Gageite, saying,

[15] 12. Make thyself more strong (for if ye be cast down they that trouble us will rejoice at it) be thou as stubborn as an old boar, harden thine heart, turn thou not to the right hand nor to the left, regard not thou their resolves,[12] their addresses, their complaints, their protests, their compliments, their flatteries, their soothings nor their threatenings.

13. But enter thou into them as the Devil entered into the herd of swine,[13] make their yoke more grievous,[14] my Grandfather corrected them with rods, but I will chastise them with scourges,[15] mine eye shall not spare them, neither will I have pity, but will recompence their ways upon their heads, that they may be a portion for the Canadians and the Quebeckites.[16]

14. For have we not heretofore nursed a brood of vipers in our bosom, that in time will gnaw out even our very vitals?

15. For who is he, what king or what nation shall be able to deliver them out of mine hand?

16. Nevertheless it came to pass about this time, that OCCUN-NEOCOGEECOCOCACHEECACHEECADUNGO,[17] the great king of the half tribe of the Chillissquasquadungo nation, the scalpers, whose habitations are in the uttermost parts of the land, in the mountains, in the forests, in the dens, caverns, and in the wigwams thereof,

17. And who were famous of old in the land of the Ohio, when the Gageites fled before them,[18] who were expert in their rifles, in [16] their bows and their arrows, their knives and their tomahawks, and who could take off the hairy scalp equal to any French tonsor in the land, heard of the things which were come to pass, and how that the heathen threatened their brethren the men of New England,

18. That he sent runners unto them, and said, Fret not thyselves because of the ungodly, for they shall soon be cut down like the grass, and be withered, even as the green herb.[19]

19. For behold, brethren, we have kindled a fire, and danced around it, and

set with our breech on the ground, and we be ready to paint our faces, disfigure our brows, and come by the light of the moon and help ye, we will cause your enemies to flee before ye, like the arrow from the bow, for did not one chase a thousand, and two put ten thousand to flight?[20]

20. For surely the wild buck knoweth no bounds, the bear laugheth at chains, the tyger will not be restrained, neither doth the fox regard an hedge, for free we were born and free we will remain.[21]

21. Why then do the heathen so furiously rage together, and why do the Britons imagine a vain thing?[22]

22. For lo the king's of the earth are gathered together, from one end thereof to the other, they stand up, and seem mad, and the rulers take counsel together, against the Lord and against his people, saying,[23]

[17] 23. Let us break their charters asunder, and cast away their liberties from them.[24]

24. And the men of New England sent messengers, and presents and thanks to Occunneocogeecococacheecacheecadungo and their brethren, and said bye and bye, only be ye ready.

25. Lay your thumbs on the feathers of your arrows, your fingers under the strings, and your left hands to the bow and stand up.

26. Now the name of Occunneocogeecococacheecacheecadungo's mother is not yet found out.

27. Now Jeremiah, the son of the prophet, gat himself up on high, and climbed on the top of Liberty Tree,[25] and sat there from the morning until the evening and said,

28. Behold, yonder I see a dark cloud like unto a large sheet rise from the NORTH,[26] big with oppression and desolation, and the four corners thereof are held by four great beasts, BUTE,[27] MANSFIELD,[28] BERNARD and HUTCHINSON,[29]

29. Carrying a large swarm like unto locusts of sycophants, commissioners, duty gatherers; custom-house officers, searchers, tide waiters, placemen, and pensioners innumerable.

30. The bastards and spurious breed of noblemen, and the children of harlots, enveloped in smoke, and big with destruction, and they seem as it were moving on toward the westward guided by the light of the star wormwood.

[18] 31. Moreover, I see Mordecai, the Benjamite, standing ready with his rod to give it the electrical shock, that it may burst with vengeance on their devoted heads.

32. And I heard a voice say unto Mordecai, Son of man, these are the four beasts that imagine mischief, and devise wicked counsel, in whom is the spirit of the evil one, and who spread lying reports throughout the land of Britain.[30]

33. And these are the extortioners and collectors of taxes that causeth the kingdom to pass away, and the glory thereof to vanish.

34. Now Mordecai, the Benjamite, watched them narrowly, and followed them with his eyes afar off, neither would he let them depart out of his sight.

35. Howbeit the men of Boston waited patiently the event,[31] for they put their trust in the Lord of Hosts, in the Congress, in themselves and in Occunneocogeecococacheecacheecadungo; for they said, Two is better than one, and a fourfold cord is not easily broken.[32]

36. Now it came to pass while the Gageites abode in the land of the Bostonites, they day by day committed iniquity, they made great clattering with their sackbutts, their psalteries, their dulcimers, bands of music, and vain parade.[33]

37. And they drummed with their drums, and piped with their pipes, making mock [19] fights, and running too and fro like shitepokes on the muddy shore.

38. Moreover by night they abused the watchmen on duty, and the young men, the children of Boston by the way side, making mouths at them, calling them Yankeys,[34] shewing their posteriors, and clapping their hands thereon.

39. And it provoked the young men, and they said unto Aminadab, we cannot bear this, these seven times they have vexed us, for they gape upon us with their mouths, as it were a ramping and a roaring lion.

40. Now therefore speak unto Jedediah the priest that he would blow the rams horns and the conch shells, that we may go and smite the heathen, O, that he would give us leave to play with them!

41. But Jedediah the priest answered, and said, Nay, my sons, let us bear with them yet seventy and seven times, for behold how good and joyful a thing it is, for brethren to dwell together in unity.[35]

42. Only be of good courage and strong; pluck up your hearts, dread not nor be afraid,[36] hold up your heads and look like young unicorns, for they are a nation void of counsel, neither is there any understanding in them.[37]

43. They shall be rewarded according to their deeds, and according to the wickedness of their own inventions,[38] they shall be recom[20]pensed after the works of their own hands,[39] they shall be paid that they have deserved, our adversaries shall be clothed with shame, and they shall cover themselves with their own confusion as with a cloak.

44. And the people said, Be it so, and they were made easy.

45.[40] Now it came to pass, when the Gageites had received succour, they prepared to go against the city, in which were men of valour, and old women and children, and the mothers of children, and grandmothers the mothers of mothers.

46. And they brought their battering rams, and their cannon whose mouths were of the diameter of a cubit, and whose throats were like unto open sepulchres, and which bellowed out fire and smoak and saltpetre and brimstone.

47. And they planted them on the neck of the Bostonites, and they laid siege against it, and built a fort and bulwarks, and cast a mount, and set the camp against it, and laid engines of war against it round about.[41]

48. And their ships, even their mighty ships of war, with their iron tiers, their pride and their boast, whose masts were of the stately cedars of Lebanon, and the huge pine from the Norwegian hills, surrounded the coasts round about,

so that the ships of the merchants that came to traffick from the isles afar off, could not enter,[42]

[21] 49. And they jested one to another, and made mouths, and squinted with their eyes, and said let us cut off the communication between the city and country, and pinch them by famine, and they will surely give up and fall a prey into our hands.

50. Now their brethren in the country, in the towns, and in the villages thereof, had divers town meetings, and they communed amongst themselves, and sent messengers unto their brethren in the city, and said,

51. Be of good comfort, come thou over to us, thou and thy wives and thy children and thy substance, and all that thou hast, and fare as we fare until we see what the Lord will do for you.

52. For behold are not our barns full, and are there not wheat and rye and Indian corn and buckwheat on our threshing floors, why then should ye abide in the city?

53. For if ye tarry, and destruction cometh upon the city, blame us not; we will wash our hands of you, for ye shall not make a covenant with the heathen for us, for their God is not as our God, even our enemies being judges.[43]

54. Now the people reasoned one with another, and said, Shall we go?

55. Howbeit, the elders of the city said unto them, Wait patiently, let us first send unto our brethren at the Congress, peradventure they will counsel us for our good.

[22] 56. And the people said, Make haste and send.

57. Now Jedediah the priest, the son of Eliphalet,[44] and Aminadab and Obadiah and Nathan and Reuben, and Zechariah and Pelatiah, and Caleb, and Ehud the son of Gera,[45] and Phineas the son of Eleazer,[46] and Othniel[47] Caleb's younger brother, and Jeremiah and Ezekiel, and Jonathan the son of Ebenezer,

58. Select men that were not minded to speak evil of another,[48] no, not even of Thomas their adversary, stood by the entry of the gate near the threshold of Thomas the Gageite.

59. And it was about the tenth hour of the day, according to the dial of Ahaz, and said,

CHAP. III.

How long wilt thou plague the people, and wilt not let them alone, for lo hast thou not made a tumult in the land, and is not the alarm gone forth among the people?

2. For surely the incongruity of thine, and thy people's proceedings, justly causeth jealousy, for thinkest thou, we and the people of this land are stocks, stones, and statues, or creatures of no sensibility?

3. For behold, have not thy soldiers wrought wickedness in the land, and vexed the young men, and abused them by the way side, making mouths at them, and grinning like monkeys?

The First Book of the American Chronicles of the Times 61

4. Moreover have ye not raised ramparts and bulwarks on our Neck?

5. Now therefore, we pray thee, desist from such abominations; these things are not right, for the young men's blood beginneth to rise, neither can they bear with it long.

[24] 6. For when one churneth milk it bringeth forth butter, and he that wringeth his nose causeth blood to come out, so he that forceth wrath bringeth forth strife.[1]

7. If thou hast been foolish in lifting thyself up, and if thou hast thought foolishly, lay thine hand upon thy mouth;[2] better is a little with peace than a great pension, and be called a lord with the curses and imprecations of the people upon thine head.

8. He that ruleth his own mind is better than he that winneth a city.

9. A little city and a few old women in it, and a great king sent against it, and compassed it about, and builded forts against it; fye, fye, better is wisdom than honour.[3]

> Honour's a puff of noisy breath,
> Yet men expose their blood;
> And venture everlasting death,
> To gain that airy good.[4]
>   Long metre.

10. Then answered Thomas and said, Take from me the noise of thy songs, For I will not hear the melody of thy viols.[5]

11. Nevertheless they said unto him, For what cause did ye come into this land? Have ye not stopped the harbour, and blocked up our ports, so that the ships from Tarshish[6] and the isles afar off may not enter, and the way side to hinder our brethren in the country from bringing their produce, the daily provisions, [25] the necessaries for the sick and feeble, for the old people and the young children, and for the labouring men?

12. And their sacks of corn, their eggs, their butter, their cheese, their potatoes, their wild fowl, their pigs and their beeves, their sheep, their venison, and their poultry, and to bring a famine in the city, that the people may die with want, and steal away our name as thou hast stolen our powder?

13. But Thomas answered, Beware of murmuring and all manner of grumblings.

14. Howbeit Obadiah lifted up his voice and spake, and said,

15. Wherefore should the names of our fathers be taken away from among his family? We have a possession, an inheritance among the brethren of our fathers.

16. Forty years was Moses and the children of Israel in the wilderness of Zin;[7] our fathers and brethren have been in possession of this wilderness of America fourscore and forty years.

17.[8] The Lord our God brought us into this land to shun the persecutions of thy people, and yet thou art come to persecute us; yea, more and more, did he not root out many of the Indian nations before us that were greater and mightier than we?

18. A land in which are rivers of water, and fountains that spring out of the vallies, rocks and hills.

[26] 19. A land of wheat and barley, of vineyards and fig trees, pomegranates and pompions, a land of fish and oil, olive and honey, a land wherein we eat bread without scarcity.

20. Neither do we lack any thing therein; a land whose stones are iron, out of whose mountains are dug gold, and whose pebbles are diamonds.

21. Then spake Thomas, and said, Where the word of the king is, there is power, and who shall say unto him, What doest thou?[9] for out of the king's lips proceed justice and wisdom.

22. Because sentence against an evil work (the destruction of the TEA CHEST) be not speedily executed, therefore the hearts of the men of Boston is fully set in them to imagine evil.[10]

23. But Pelatiah spake and said, Thy tender mercies are cruelties; it is better to die by the sword than by famine; it is better to trust in the Lord than to put any confidence in princes.[11]

24. Now Thomas waxed wroth and opened his mouth once more, and said,

25. Wherefore do ye turn aside unto vain jangling, pretending to be teachers of the law, yet understanding neither what they say, nor what they affirm, but doting about questions and words, whereof cometh strife, railings, evil surmisings, perverse disputings of [27] men's corrupt minds, and destitute of the truth?[12]

26. Shall not your folly be made manifest unto all men, even as was that of Jannes and Jambres who withstood Moses?[13]

27. Now arose Phineas,[14] a man of Suffolk, the son of Eleazer, who was of a warm disposition, yet nevertheless prudent, whose face was ruddy,[15] and whose countenance was like the sun at noonday,[16] the captain of the host, a mighty man, and a warrior from his youth, he was the chief of the thirty champions of New England, he killed four she bears, and slew three giants, the sons of Anak,[17] in single combat, and brought away their heads, and his mother's name was * * * * * * * * *.

28. Moreover he was a captain of old at the siege of Louisbourgh,[18] when it fell into the hands of the men of New England, and said,

29. Why boasteth thyself, thou tyrant, that thou canst do mischief?

30. For there is no king can be saved by the multitude of an host, neither is any mighty man delivered by much strength.[19]

31. For many dogs are come about us, and the counsel of the wicked lay siege against us, deal not so madly, set not up your horn on high, and speak not with a stiff neck,[20] lest ye be bruised with a rod of iron, and broken in pieces like a potter's vessel.[21]

[28] 32. For thou thyself imagines mischief in thine heart, and stirreth up

strife all the day long. For it is not an open enemy that hath done us this wrong, for then we could not have borne it.[22]

33. But this land and those possessions are ours, and as the Lord liveth, though thy strength were ten times more abundant, like unto the host of Pharoah, or even like unto that of Senacherib,[23] thou shall not dispossess us, for there be no Esau's among us, neither do we mean to sell our birthright for a dish of TEA.[24]

34. For the Congress will stand to their cause, and bring forth their strong reasons; they shall be like unto trees planted by the water side, which will bring forth their fruit in due season.[25]

35. Now Thomas waxed more and more wroth, and spake unto Phineas, and said,

36. The pride of thine heart hath deceived thee, thou that dwelleth in the clefts of the rocks, though thou exalt thyself with the eagle, and though thou set thy nest among the stars, thence will I bring thee down, and all the men of thy Congress, and of thy confederacy, will I bring down even unto the border.[26]

37. Nevertheless Phineas answered, and said, Pride goeth before destruction, and an haughty spirit before a fall,[27] it is an honour for a man to cease from strife, but fools will be meddling.[28]

[29] 38. Nevertheless, seeing ye are for blood, we will make our arrows drunk with blood, and our swords shall eat flesh,[29] and the word shall be THE SWORD OF THE LORD AND OF OLIVER.

39. Now behold Thomas, sirnamed the Gageite, turned his back upon them, nor vouchsafed them any further argumentation, for he was an haughty man, and a great snuff taker.

40. Moreover he lacked wherewithal to make them an answer.

41. Now Matherius Cottonius,[30] the former high priest, being dead, and sleeping with his fathers, and all New England had lamented him, and mourned for him, and buried him in the Old South, in his own sepulchre, and in his own city, after he had put away the soothsayers, the sorcerers, the witches, and Balaam the wizzard,[31] out of the land.

42.[32] That his successor, Jedediah the priest (not having the gift of prophesy, and moreover, somewhat, doubtful how the matter might terminate betwixt the Gageites and themselves) asked counsel, but he was not answered by dreams, by visions, by the beating of the pulse, by urine, nor yet by prophets.

43. That Jedediah spake unto Aminadab and Obadiah, saying,

44. Be there not still remaining, in all the land of New England, a prophetess, a [30] cunning old woman, whom men call a witch, and who hath in times past foretold divers things, which have come to pass?

45. And Obadiah answered and said, Yea verily, behold there be one left, that abideth in the suburbs, one whom I know full well, a woman that is a charmer, that hath a familiar spirit, and knoweth all things which shall come to pass.

46. Then Jedediah, the priest, changed himself, and put on other raiment, and he went and took Aminadab and Obadiah with him, and they came to the woman by night.

47. And it came to pass that Jedediah knocked at her door with his staff, and said unto her, I pray thee let me come in unto thee, and let me partake of thy secrets.

48. And the woman opened her gate, and Jedediah went in unto her, and kissed her, and Obadiah and Aminadab remained without, and she spread a table, and she put there on, and said, Surely thou shalt eat with me, and Jedediah sat down and did eat with her, and drank wine.

49. Now Obadiah waxed exceedingly jealous, howbeit he held his peace, while Aminadab knew not what these things meant.

50. Now all this while Aminadab and Obadiah remained outside the door of the house, and it rained and grew cold, and Obadiah lifted the latch of the door, and they entered in and saluted the woman, and sat by the fire and warmed themselves.

[31] 51. And the woman said unto Jedediah, Are these thy friends? And he answered and said unto her, Yea, verily; and she made them welcome, and they sat down, and did eat and drink.

52. And Jedediah said unto her, Now know I of a truth, indeed, that thou art a charmer, and hast a kind familiar spirit, that thou art a regarder of the times, a marker of the flying of fowls, a witch, and converseth with the dead, that thou art highly favoured, that thou canst divine, canst do and tell of things that are mystical, obscure, abstruse and remote from conception.

53. Now therefore I pray thee conjecture unto me by the familiar spirit, and bring me him up whom I shall name unto thee.

54. But the woman, whose name was Carey,[33] was amazed and afraid, and she said unto him, How is it that ye ask such things of me, seeing I have not practised them these fourscore years, behold thou knowest what Matherius Cottonius hath done, how that he hath destroyed the sorcerers, the soothsayers, and the witches out of the land, wherefore then seekest thou to take me in a snare to tell of me, and cause me to die?[34]

55. Then Jedediah, the priest, said unto her, Knowest thou not, sister Carey, old things are done away, and all things are become new,[35] that without thy help we may be all lost.

[32] 56. And she said, If thou wilt keep it secret, and sware unto me, then will I satisfy all thy desires.

57. And it came to pass that Jedediah did so, and Mother Carey was therewith content; but Obadiah grumbled within himself, yet nevertheless spake he not a word.

58.[36] Now Mother Carey said, Whom shall I bring up unto thee?

59. Then Jedediah answered and said, Bring me up OLIVER CROMWELL.[37]

60.[38] And when the woman saw Oliver, she cried with a loud voice, and spake unto Jedediah, saying, Why hast thou deceived me; I took thee for Obadiah, but thou art Jedediah, the priest, that hath done this thing, and why hast thou constrained me to call up such a monster?

61. And he said unto her, Sister Carey, my charmer, be not afraid, the necessity of the times maketh it necessary; what seest thou, what fashion is he of?

62. And she answered, An old man, with a high crowned hat, cometh up, with whiskers, having on a brigandine or coat of mail, a breast plate of boldness, a two edged sword in his hand, half boots on his legs, his belt stuck round with pistols, like the devil in a thorn bush, and a face like unto the face of a rhinoceros.[39]

[33] 63. Then Jedediah knew that it was Oliver, and he inclined his face to the ground, and bowed himself, likewise did Aminadab and Obadiah.

64. And Cromwell saluted them and said, GRACE BE UNTO YOU, wherefore have you disquieted me to bring me up?

CHAP. IV.

THEN answered Jedediah, and said, Thy sons are in great distress, for the Gageites are come into the land, they are preparing for our destruction, and to make war against thy people, therefore thy counsel and spirit are much wanted at this time, for unto whom can we seek for succour but unto thee, next to the Lord of Hosts?

2. Moreover there be some eunuchs of the tribe of Levi,[1] Coo-r-ites, the Friendly Addresser,[2] R---g--n the *pretended* Letter Presser;[3] that want to divide the people into factions, and who go about like unto owls by night privily, through the city, in the high ways, in the streets, at the corners, in the alleys, lanes, by-ways, and in the secret places thereof.

3. Haranguing the ignorant, and making scandalous pamphlets,[4] and newspapers, against the Congress, and against the proceedings thereof, endeavouring to set it at nought, and against thy people, and blaspheme thy name.

[36] 4. Therefore be not thou angry with thy sons, we pray thee, neither be thou displeased with our sister Carey, who stands trembling and weeping before thy face, for behold she hath done this thing at my desire, and that good may come out of evil, therefore let all thy vengeance, if any, fall upon the head of Obadiah, for he shewed her unto me, and brought me hither, but be not thou angry with thy sons, we pray thee, for thy name is *precious in their mouths.*

5. Then Cromwell, looking pleasantly on the woman, took her by the hand, and said unto her, Comfort thy heart, daughter Carey, thou that art the daughter of the mother of all witches, for no harm shall come unto thee, and the woman made a low curtesy unto him, and dried up her tears, and her fears vanished away, and he said unto Obadiah, Obadiah, thou hast done well.

6. Then spake Oliver unto Jedediah, and said, Regard not thou these sons of slander, for they be sycophants and understrappers; they be like unto monkeys grinning at a lion, like unto puppies barking at the moon; they are wolves in sheep's clothing.[5]

7. For these things do they to serve themselves, that they may be taken notice of and rewarded by their master, even as the traitors Bernard and Hutchinson are rewarded, and who will say unto them, Well done, ye good [37] and faithful servants, come thou, and take the mitre on thine head, and be a BISHOP; and come thou unto me, for thou shalt be the KING's PRINTER.

8. Now mark what I shall say unto you, Jedediah, I will deal with their superiors and not with them, and notwithstanding their utmost efforts to enslave you, the lamp of liberty shall still burn with purified oil, like unto that which ran down Aaron's beard,[6] not made of blubber, but pure virgin oil, and triumphantly shall ye rejoice in the smell thereof.

9. And although they make a jest of our divine charter,[7] our blessed Magna Charta, yet shall it not be prostituted to wrap up their poisonous TEA.

10. But I will cause the lining of their TEA CHESTS to be cast up, and converted into musket balls, and the chests themselves shall be metamorphosed into a whipping post and pillory for Bernard and Hutchinson.

11. And the remainder thereof shall be transformed into tar barrels, and into traps to catch the Coo--r-ites, the R-g-n-ites, and other half priced political rats; for have not I spoken it? saith OLIVER.

12. Then spake Jedediah, and lifted up his hands and eyes, and said, O how highly favoured are we thy sons, that it be permitted that thou, our great Lord and mighty Pro[38]tector, regardest his children, who hatest hypocrisy and dissimulation, whose conscience is always void of offence,[8] who refused an earthly crown that thou mightest be rewarded with a crown of glory, who art ambitious only for the glory of the King of Kings; thou whose consummate fortitude, magnanimity and prudence, whose great and divine talents were bestowed from above, to answer wise purposes and happy events, how didst thou raise the fading glory and dying reputation of the British nation, beyond the highest pitch of Roman greatness;[9] the heads of kings and princes were but as snow balls in thine hands, and thou hustled powers, principalities, and kingdoms as in a cap; thou became the dread and terror of the nations round about;[10] thou swayed the sceptre of this terrestrial universe, and held the balance of power in thine own hands,[11] thou broughtest true religion to the highest pitch, and banished enthusiasm, fanaticism, high church bigotry, popish superstition, and pretenders to saintship, out of the land;[12] thou shook his Holiness's hair, made the tripple crown of the great dragon to totter, thou madest the papal cap to fall off from his hoary pate, thou pulled the purple robe from off his shoulders, and made thereof a carpet for the soles of thy shoes, and left him as bare as an unfledged woodpecker;[13] thou suffered not the [39] haughty king of France to enjoy his boasted vain title, but permitted him to be called only the simple

French king;[14] the invincible proud Spaniard[15] thou humbled in the dust, and made their Donships, Don Falsey Benabio, and Don Diego Surly Phiz, their ministers, as submissive as spaniels; thou despised their treasure, their silver and their gold, and sunk their galleons in the depths of the sea;[16] the sly Hogan Mogans of the United Provinces trembled at thy nod, they besought thy friendship, and their High Mightynesses became the poor and distressed states;[17] the strong holds and impenetrable castles of the piratical Algerines became but as sport and pastime in thine hands, and the ships of all nations thou made to lower their pride, pay homage, and bow down to thy all conquering flag;[18] thou settest up whatsoever thou pleasest, and pullest down whomsoever thou wilt.

13. Now behold, while Jedediah was speaking, CROMWELL smiled on him, and it pleased him, insomuch that it made his heart glad and leap for joy, for he was not proof against flattery, but rejoiced to hear his own actions and great atcheivements praised and extolled, even unto the skies.

14. And it came to pass, when he had twirled his whiskers, and stroked his beard, he said unto him, He that is not for us is against us,[19] what meaneth Thomas the Usurper.

[40] 15. Behold I will shortly let him know to his sorrow, what it is to disturb the pious ashes of them that sleepeth, to threaten my beloved people, and to affront the majesty of OLIVER; for in seven nights will I appear in a vision before him, face to face.

16. Hearken therefore, Jedediah, to what I shall speak in thine ear, take counsel of me, and suffer not your spirits to flag, be thou and our people resolute, give back not one inch, and, if so be ye are constrained to fight with them, behold I will be in the midst of you, you shall find me in the centre, in the wings, and in the fore front of the battle, and when you find me flinch, then execrate the name and memory of OLIVER.

17. For I will break those chains in sunder which have been prepared to shackle you,[20] and they shall moulder away like clay, and you shalt surely prove victorious, and triumph over your enemies; am not I your Lord Protector; for history cannot point out, neither can the Chronicles tell wherein a true born Oliverian ever flinched or forsook his cause; witness my prowess at the memorable battle of Marsdon Moor.[21]

18. Moreover I will cause the heads of Johnny the Butetite, and Haman the Northite,[22] to be lopped from off their shoulders, even as the limb of a tree is lopped off, and they shall be hanged on a gallows fifty cubits [41] high, and they shall remain on the walls of the gates of Britain as a memorial, even as I was ofttimes wont to serve traitors of old, and as rebels are served.[23]

19. Then were the hearts of Jedediah and Aminadab and Obadiah glad, and they bowed seven times unto OLIVER, and fell with their faces to the ground.

20. And OLIVER said unto them, Rise and stand up on your feet like men, and go ye into the city and tell my people, you have this night seen the face of Cromwell their Lord Protector, which no man hath seen these six score years.[24]

21. Moreover tell Phineas, the captain of the host, the son of Eleazer, be strong and whet up his plow shares into swords, and his pruning hooks into spears.[25]

22. Tell Occunneocogeecococacheecacheecadungo, my brother, fill up his quiver, and stand up and tarry till I come, and take ye this in thine hand and proclaim it through the city, and throughout all the land of New England; farewel, while I make an excursion to the mansions of them that sleepeth, and awake and rouse up my faithful Fairfax,[26] Lambert,[27] and the rest of my brave warriors: THE LORD PROSPER YOU; GRACE BE UNTO YOU.

23. And he departed out of their sight in a terrible whirlwind, and they saw him no [42] more that time, neither knew they where or which way he went.

24. Now as soon as Venus, the evening star, began to be dull and drowsy, they took their leave of Mother Carey, and Jedediah, the priest, shook her by the hand and stroked her, and kissed her, and looked wishfully on her, and because the night was cold and rainy, she covered his shoulders with her newest under garment, and she smiled on him, and they went their way.

25. Howbeit, Obadiah went on grumbling and sorrowful, nor yet opened he his mouth.

26. And it came to pass, as they were on their way, Aminadab pondered these things in his heart.

27. Now behold when they were come into the city, that on the next day, and in the morning thereof, Jedediah, the priest, caused all the people to be assembled, and they came from all quarters and assembled themselves together, and from the suburbs, and from the country, and the villages and towns round about, a very great multitude.

28. And he said, Listen, brethren, I pray you, that ye may understand, for behold our Lord Protector OLIVER hath appeared, and hath commanded me, his servant, to proclaim this unto you; and he pulled from under his mantle a roll of parchment (for [43] he wore no cassock nor band) and he said, Give attention, O all ye people; and the people remained silent, and he read therein with a loud voice, and spake unto them through a fisherman's trumpet, and said,

By his HIGHNESS OLIVER CROMWELL, the most Invincible, Puissant, Invulnerable, Magnanimous, and Evangelical, LORD PROTECTOR of the Commonwealth of the Province of the Massachusetts Bay, in New England, and the Territories thereunto depending, Generalissimo, Chancellor, and Lord High Admiral of the same,

A PROCLAMATION.[28]

WHEREAS I have received information, that his Excellency Thomas, surnamed the Gageite, otherwise called the Usurper, on the 28th day of September last did most daringly, wantonly, abominably, wickedly, atrociously and devilishly, and without my knowledge, allowance, approbation, instruction or consent first had and obtained, and without my name, and the imperial signet of the Commonwealth affixed thereunto,[29] [44] did presume, and *ipso facto* issue forth and publish a most diabolical and treasonable proclamation, in order to delude my true and faithful subjects, and cause them to swerve from the right way, and to throw off their allegiance unto me their true lawful, rightful Lord, and Sovereign Protector, to the great detriment and disquiet of their consciences, by endeavouring to establish the doctrine of the arrant whore of Rome, as well their worldly interest, by commanding my loving subjects to pay the taxes, and other duties and customs of the land, into the hands of a tool of his own appointment.

NOW KNOW YE, That for divers good causes and considerations, which shall be made manifest in due time, I have thought fit, by and with the advice and consent of my trusty and well beloved cousins, generals, and council,[30] Fairfax, Ireton, Willoughby, Zankey, Skippon, Hammond, Rainsborough, Pride, Lambert, Coote, Venables, Broghill, Hewson, Abbot, Reynolds, Ewer, Lilburn, Fleetwood, Desborough, Harrison, Blake, Gibbons, Marsh, and Jones, to issue this my proclamation, and by the authority aforesaid, do highly disapprove and contemn the above recited proclamation, hereby strictly charging and enjoining, and exhorting all Selectmen, judges, justices of the peace, sheriffs, collectors of taxes, constables, and [45] all whom it may concern, to disregard, reject and utterly refuse paying any obedience whatsoever thereunto, but that they do forthwith pay all monies, so received or may hereafter receive, by virtue of their offices, into the hands of my faithful, trusty cousin, and worthy collector, colonel Bradshaw,[31] whom I have appointed for that purpose, until my further pleasure in the premises be made known, as they will answer the contrary at their peril, or otherwise as they regard my blessing.

AND WHEREAS it is highly expedient, to the intent therefore, that the perpetrator of such unheard of and unparalleled piece of effrontery, and misdemeanor, should be apprehended and brought to condign punishment, and that it may be a caution to all and every one, not to commit the like trespass, I do hereby further, by the advice and consent of the council aforesaid, promise, that if any person or persons shall apprehend and deliver, or cause to be delivered, over to the Selectmen of Boston, or to Colonel J. H-----k, Moderator and Chairman of the Provincial Congress,[32] the said Thomas, surnamed the Gageite, otherwise named the Usurper, such person or persons shall thereupon have, and receive, out of the profits arising from the sale of the TEA, a reward of ONE SHILLING OLD TENOR,[33] over [46] and above what the charter of the province allows in such cases made and provided.

GIVEN under my hand, and the great and imperial signet of the Commonwealth of the province of New England, at Boston, the 27th day of October, in the year of our Lord one thousand seven hundred and seventy-four, and in or about the tenth year of our SOVEREIGN LORD PERSECUTION, by the GRACE of SATAN, KING of TYRANNY, CONFUSION and POPERY, DEFENDER of the ROMISH FAITH, &c.

OLIVER CROMWELL.

By his Highness's command,
    BRADSHAW, Secretary.

GRACE BE UNTO YOU.

CHAP. V.

AND it came to pass when Jedediah had made an end of reading the proclamation, that there was joy manifest and visible in the countenances of all the people, and they gave a great shout, and the rumour thereof spread abroad throughout all the land, and behold that day will forever be kept as an holy day on account of the new birth of Oliver.

2. Now every man was ready to help his neighbour,[1] and said unto his brother, Our Lord Protector hath appeared, for behold Jedediah the priest hath seen him face to face, and talked with him, now therefore be strong, they shall be as nothing, and the men that war against thee as a thing of nought.

3. Moreover every man's sword was as sharp as a barber's razor.

4.[2] Now it came to pass about this time, that there came a ship from the land of Britain afar off, with merchandize and TEA, and cast her anchor in the harbour of the Marylandites.

[48] 5. And behold, Joseph, and James, and Anthony, the merchants (for it was their ship) committed a trespass against the people.

6. For they paid unto the king's collector, the duty thereof unknown to the people, even the duty for the TEA.

7. Howbeit the Marylandites were like watchmen on the towers, they kept a good look out (for the spirit of liberty, of watchfulness and freedom, went throughout the land) and they assembled themselves together, and consulted, and they brought Joseph and James and Anthony, the merchants, before them.

8. And they said unto them, Wherefore have you committed this iniquity in the land? behold, ye be but three, and ye be not able to stand before this multitude.

9. Now they were sore afraid and dismayed, and said unto the men of Maryland, We have indeed sinned against the people of the land.

10. Nevertheless, suffer us we pray ye, to make an atonement, and moreover that we make a sacrifice of the TEA, and a burnt offering of the ship.

11. And the men of Maryland said unto them, Seeing ye are minded to make a free-will offering, and not of turtle doves, nor young pidgeons, or fatted calves, of rams, nor he-goats (which things will not atone for a sin offering) we will

therefore suffer ye to do even as [49] ye have said, to purge the iniquity out of the land, and that the land be no longer defiled.

12. And it came to pass, that Joseph and James and Anthony went their way, and they took firebrands in their hands, and they went and climbed up on board the ship, and they entered in and they set fire thereto, and blew it with their mouths, before the face of the multitude.

13. And the flames thereof, and the sparks, and the smoke ascended upwards, and the south wind blew them onward towards the NORTH, and the lower part of the ship sunk in the depths of the waters.

14. And they kneeled on their knees, and begged pardon, and smote their breasts, and said, We have sinned, we pray ye therefore have mercy upon us.

15. And they vowed a vow before the face of all the congregation, that they would never commit the like trespass again, for their hearts were heavy, and they were sore troubled, neither would they do so any more.

16. So the people of the land believed them, and took pity on them, and had compassion on them, and forgave them for that time.

17. Now it came to pass, that in the evening, when the Bostonian men of the Grand Congress,[3] Thomas the Cushingite,[4] the Adamites,[5] and Robert the Painite,[6] had returned home and come into the city and unto [50] their own homes, that their wives and their little ones received them tenderly, and clung about their necks for joy, and kissed them.

18. And the people came from all quarters, and they assembled themselves like bees in an hive, and greeted them, and made them welcome.

19. And they made bonfires, and they illuminated their houses, and the candles which were of spermaceti, and lights shone with unusual lustre and brightness, and the smell thereof was like unto the frankincense and myrrh of Cassia, the same which the queen of Sheba brought unto Solomon.[7]

20. And they fired their guns and discharged their pieces nineteen times in a minute, exceeding far away in quickness the fire of those that are undeservedly and falsely called regulars, and who are but as recruits, compared unto the men of Boston.

21. And the bells of the steeples, of the churches, and of the Old South, rang for joy, that the city looked even like unto a city of magic lanthorns, neither was the like ever seen in the land of New England since they took the strong hold of Louisburgh.[8]

22. Insomuch that it dazzled the eyes of the Jacobites, the Governmentites, and the Gageites afar off, and it made them squint and look awry.

23. And behold they squint, and write egregious pamphlets, and press them in the letter press, even unto this day.

[51] 24. Now Thomas surnamed the Gageite looked out of a window and beheld these things afar off, and he said unto Simon, his chaplain,[9] What meaneth all this?

25. But behold Simon was inebriated (he loved carousing) and was not in a condition to inform him, for he squinted more than them all, and objects multiplied, and magnified in his sight, for he viewed them obliquely, obtusely, acutely and horizontally.

> For he always stood firm to his text,
> And believ'd there was virtue in wine;
> And he thought that a glass of the next
> Wou'd make wit still the brighter to shine.
> By wine he replenish'd his veins,
> And made his religion to real;
> Then fancy'd the lights, like his brains,
> Turn'd like a Copernican wheel.
> For he, like the vicar, the test of good liquor,
> Call'd boy—bring a glass of the best,
> Faith ! mind not their rout, let their candles burn out.
> And then we may safely go rest. [10]

26. Howbeit Thomas, willing to satisfy his fears, called for Monsieur De la Cutta de Bearda,[11] his tonsor and valet de chambre, and said unto him, Tell me the cause thereof?

27. Then spake Monsieur De la Cutta de Bearda, (as well as he could) and said, Owe Monsieur Excelancy, de gentlemans of de Grand Congre, be comee home a, to de [52] town a, and de peoper a make a de great a luminasiong, and make a de chandelier burn a, and make de fire a, and fire de great gunna, for aw dat, and for de joi of dat.

28. Now it came to pass, when he understood the meaning thereof, he fell with his face on his couch, and he swooned away, and he fell asleep in a deep trance, and the soul of Thomas departed from him for a short space of time.

29. And he dreamed a dream, and behold he saw Cromwell standing before him, and he grinned at him, and stamped with his foot, and shook his head as if he would bite him, and looked horribly on him, and threatened him, and said unto him, Depart hence thou Usurper, and let me see thy face no more.

30. Insomuch, that when he awoke, the drops of cold sweat fell from off him, his tongue hung out of his mouth, his limbs shook, his countenance was sometimes pallid and anon would change colour like unto a chameleon, and his bones rattled within his skin.

31. And he cried out with a hollow murmuring voice, O, Oliver, Oliver thou art too terrible, I cannot bear thy stern looks, for thou art an over match for Lucifer himself.

32. Now behold, the next day Thomas was seized with a trepidation, he looked sorrowful, and was seemingly in great tribulation, he would neither eat nor drink, he would not open his mouth to any one, neither did [53] any one dare to speak unto him, nor comfort him.

33. Insomuch that those of his own houshold marvelled greatly, and his

soldiers stood amazed and quitted their stations, and some there were who deserted, so that the drummers were commanded to beat the tattoo, to warn them to their quarters.

34. Howbeit, Simon his chaplain, a man of a persecuting spirit, yet withal a pretender to moderation, well acquainted with the doctrine and customs of a well spread table, but a stranger to grace either before or after meat;

35. Fond of crabs, lobsters, and all kinds of fish, yet nevertheless cautious of choking himself with bones, cared little for his God, but worshipped his own belly, preferring a bottle of champaigne to a fountain of living water, and fonder of a back gammon table than a church bible.

36. When he had recovered a little from the fatigue of the last evening's vespers, being yet weary and heavy laden, having some small remains of the vertigo, he went into the chamber of Thomas and drew the curtain of the bed and spake unto him, and said,

37. Why mourn ye thus all the day long? Arise, eat, drink, and be merry, or before tomorrow's dawn thou will not have a soldier left to fight for thee, not one of thy household save me, to comfort thee, for behold, thy soldiers desert in droves, and the Philistians will surely be upon thee,[12] Thomas.

[54] 38. Then opened Thomas his eyes, and looked on him, and answered and said unto him, Oh, Simon, didst thou but know—I have this night seen—

39. Now, all this while Simon viewed him askance, and said unto him, And what hast thou seen? Not the Old Boy,[13] I hope, God forbid.

40. And Thomas spoke, and said unto him, Beloved Simon, jest me not, Oh gladly would I it had been him, for believe me, Simon, I have this night seen—

41. And Simon laughed and said, A night hag, I suppose, riding through the air, drawing a broom stick with Lapland witches,[14] or has some of mother Cary's chickens been hovering around thy brain?[15]

42. And Thomas answered and said, Oh, Simon, forbear thy jests, what mine eyes have seen are far more terrible than them all, I have seen the face of Cromwell—Oliver's—Oliver's face—

43. Then Simon said unto him, Shadows, phantoms, chimeras, bugbears, the effluvia, of a wild imagination, arise, and drink deep of the stream, and forget all your care.

44. And Thomas said unto him, My beloved Simon, my reverend chaplain, thou knowest me well—believe me then—'twas no shadow but a real substance,[16] even as thou thyself art, pray for me, I beseech thee.

[55] 45. Now Simon began to be somewhat more serious, and thought within himself it might be so, and said, I will judge not lest I be judged[17] (for he was not thoroughly satisfied concerning the doctrine of apparitions) neither was he minded to dispute the authority of the scriptures, concerning the speaking of Balaam's ass.[18]

46. Moreover he had heard of Cromwell's appearing unto Jedediah the priest, and of his proclamation, and he said unto himself, Perhaps the effevesence of

my own brain at this time may render me incapable of judging aright, for—let me see—I forget the chapter, as well as the book—but it matters not, it is somewhere.

Now Simon reasoned thus, *exempli gratia.*

Did Balaam's ass speak, or did he not? Yes, granted.

Since Balaam's ass spoke, why might not the witch of En-dor raise up Samuel,[19] did she raise up Samuel? Yes, granted.

If Samuel was a shadow only could he have had power to speak? No, not allowed.

Since Samuel was a real substance, raised by the witch of En-dor, and had power to speak, did he speak unto Saul? Yes, granted.

Seeing therefore that the principle of this hypothesis is undeniably proved, to wit, that Balaam's ass did speak, that the witch of En-dor did raise up Samuel, that Samuel did speak unto Saul, and that Samuel was not a [56] shadow but a real substance, I say, seeing they are granted, let us proceed a little farther.

Why then might not Mother Carey, by the same enchanting power and hereditary right, seeing she was the eldest daughter of Balaam the wizard, by his wife the witch of En-dor (whose name I have forgot) raise up Oliver Cromwell, did Mother Carey raise up Oliver Cromwell by virtue of her power and hereditary right? Yes, granted.

Could Oliver have avoided it, had he been so inclined? No, by no means.

If Cromwell was a shadow only, could he have had power to speak? No, not at all.

Since Cromwell was a real substance, raised by Mother Carey, and had power to speak, did he speak unto Jedediah the priest? Yes, granted.

Seeing therefore that we have converted the hypothesis into a matter of fact, without straining the text, we may therefore defy all unbelievers, critics and hypercritics, to dispute the reality of appearance.[20]

Again, feeling therefore that Mother Carey did raise Oliver, and that Oliver did speak unto Jedediah (for by the character Jedediah bears especially amongst his own people, and a priest too) I can hardly think he would lie about the matter, besides there is Oliver's proclamation wrote by his own hand, which a number of the Bostonites have sworn to, being well acquainted with his hand [57] writing and two other circumstances in favour are the date, and the freshness of the paper.[21]

I say, taking all these for facts, which they incontestably are, and deny it who can, the matter will stand thus.

Balaam's ass did speak, but he could not have spoken unless he had had something to say; the witch of En-dor did raise up Samuel, which she could not have done unless she had power, Samuel could not have spoken, if he had nothing to say, and if he had not been raised, neither could he have spoken unto Saul at all, unless Saul had been present, so Mother Carey, having power by her hereditary right, as being the eldest daughter (as I said before) of Balaam the wizard, by his wife the witch of En-dor, had power to raise Oliver; but Oliver could not have spoken unless he had something to say, and unless he had been raised, neither could he have spoken unto Jedediah, unless Jedediah had been there.

Now the inference and conclusion are these, that Oliver Cromwell, by the same power that he appeared unto Jedediah, did appear unto Thomas the Gageite, a real substance, and spoke unto him; and therefore the doctrine of apparitions are fully proved, so that it should by no means be rejected, but that we should stick up to the text, without departing from it one jot or one tittle.

46. Now spake Simon unto Thomas and said, From all evil and mischief I pray that [58] thou may be delivered, I will haste and call unto thee thy physicians, let them try the power of terrestrial medicines, and if that fails, then will I administer celestial physic, and he departed out of the chamber.

47.[22] And behold about this time there came another TEA SHIP from the land of Britain, and cast her anchor in the river of York, in the land of the Virginites, and the Sons of Liberty and the Virginia Rangers assembled themselves together, and the TEA and their TEA CHESTS ascended up in a pillar of fire and smoke, and vanished out of sight.

48. But the ship being innocent, and the owner thereof a righteous man, and knowing nought of the matter, for his sake therefore they suffered her to depart to the isles afar off.

CHAP. VI.

WHEN the king shall sit upon the throne of his kingdom, then shall he regard the law as it is written in the book, and it shall be with him, and he shall read therein all the days of his life.[1]

That he may learn to fear the Lord his God, and to keep all the words of the law and the ordinances to do them.

That his heart be not lifted up above his brethren, and that he turn not from the law, to the right hand, nor to the left, that he may prolong his days in his kingdom, he and his sons in the midst of Britain for ever.

Wherefore then dost thou strive against thy servants,[2] and put heavy tax masters over them?

Now, O king Rehoboam, did not the men of America thy servants dwell without fear, every man under his vine, and under his fig tree, from Terra Labradore unto the coast of the Georgeites, all the days of Solomon thy grandfather?[3]

[60] Did not the antient men, the Pitites,[4] that stood before Solomon thy grandfather while he yet lived, counsel thee to be kind unto the children of America, and speak loving words unto them, and please them, and they will be thy servants for ever?

But behold, O king, thou hast rejected the counsel of the old men,[5] the

Pittites, and followed that of the young men, even that of Johnny the Butite, and that of the wicked Haman the Northite.

Who said unto thee, Thy least part shall be bigger than thy grandfather's loins, make their yoke more grievous, thy grandfather corrected them with rods, but do thou, O king Rehoboam, chastise them with scorpions, then shall we trample them under our feet.[6]

Now Johnny the Butite and Haman the Northite caused Rehoboam to do evil in the sight of the Lord.

Howbeit it made the belly of the Pope to shake for joy, and his Holiness cracked his sides with laughter, for they caused Britain to sin, they encouraged the setting up groves and golden calves,[7] in the land of the Canadians and the Quebeckites,[8] and in the plains of Abraham, and dishonored the memory of the immortal Wolf.[9]

And Rehoboam walked no more in the ways of Solomon his grandfather, but walked in the ways of Louis king of France,[10] and of Carolus king of Hispania,[11] and made molten [61] images for Balaam and for Pope Gregory Hildebrand.[12]

Now, O king, do we not pour out our wealth into thy lap, and into the lap of thy beloved, even the pure gold of Ophir[13] and Portugal, and the fine silver of Mexico and Peru,[14] that hath been tried seven times in the fire? And notwithstanding thou and thy nobles be not content.

Do we not bring presents of food and raiment day by day, for thee and thy household, for thy wives, thy concubines, and thy little ones, neither be ye satisfied. Have we not covered thy face with fatness, and hast thou not great collops of fat upon thy flanks?

Dost thy hands or thy fingers work, or dost thy head assist the cunning workman? Dost thou not beget children like pismires? Dost not the beloved of thy bosom breed like a rabbit? And are not thy offspring as numerous as the coneys among the stoney rocks? Thy heart be not satisfied.

Now, O king, what heart can desire more? Even Solomon thy grandfather in all his glory (of these things) did not excel thee.

Wherefore then dost thou lift up the sceptre of thine indignation against us? Surely, O king, thou requitest us evil for good, for hast thou not cast upon us the furiousness of thy wrath, anger, displeasure, and trouble, and sent evil angels and hot thunder bolts amongst us?

[62] Moreover, thou hast not regarded our messengers nor our petitions, and hast disregarded our supplications, neither hast thou honoured our ambassador.[15] Didst thou not take from Mordecai his post, and almost stone him with stones, as was St. Stephen of old,[16] for doing that which was right in the sight of the Lord?

And hast thou not sent forth a decree, that all the world should be taxed for the God of the TEA CHEST?

Didst thou not in the days of the Stamp Act, shed the blood of our brethren like water on every side, even in the city and in the streets of Boston, so that it ran down the gutters thereof like unto the lava from the eruption of mount Etna or Vesuvius?[17]

Flee, flee, far away from us thou bastard of the Stamp Act, for doth not a burnt child dread the fire?

And yet, notwithstanding, would we not all to a man (were it the laws of our own land)[18] rather sooner agree voluntarily to burn our throats with a ladle of hot mush, our own country produce and manufacture, than have the nosle of a tea pot crammed down our throats, and scalded with the abominable and baneful exotic,[19] without our own consent?

And moreover, O king, hast thou not made a Jesuitical decree, that our half brethren the Canadians and Quebeckites fall down and worship graven images? And per[63]adventure, we and our children be commanded to fall down and worship them also.

No, we cannot persuade ourselves to disturb the ashes of our forefathers and former teachers, who were men of piety, disinterested virtue, and true catholic reformation principles, and whose doctrine make our souls to live. We cannot persuade ourselves to adopt the doctrine of passive obedience and non-resistance, we cannot apostatise, we will not, though Belzebub himself should be belwether to his holiness,[20] and stand at our gate with all his bald pated fryars, and imps of hell at his elbow, but firmly to a man resolved are we to hold fast our integrity.

For, O king, knowest thou not, we ever had a great aversion to bishops?[21]

How then can we admit a pope, cardinals, inquisitors, jesuits, confessors, fryars dominican or franciscan, capuchin monks, or the society of congregatio de propaganda,[22] cowls, hoods, habits, reliques, pardons, indulgences plenarie, dispenses, and bulla de la sancta erugada's, and devils with seven heads and ten horns?[23]

With all their trumpery of processions, ceremonious solemnities, te deums, ave marias, pennances, incense, beads, thumping, holy water, and such stuff?

No verily, we cannot abide with those that hold of superstitious vanities, for our harps we will hang up on the willow trees,[24] neither [64] will we tune our voices to chant harmonious popish vespers.

For be it known unto thee, O King Rehoboam, we well remember to have heard our mothers declare (and have we not read it in our primers)[25] concerning John Rodgers[26] minister of the gospel, the first glorious martyr, who was burnt at Smithfield, two hundred years ago and upwards, in the reign of the bloody queen Mary?

Now God forbid we should forsake the Lord to serve idolatrous Gods as doth the Canadians and Quebeckites, there shall no strange Gods come hither, neither will we worship any God, save our own.

No surely, thy servants will all to a man sooner die martyrs to the true faith than worship the God of Nafroch, neither will we be bound in chains of popery, nor fetters of superstition.

For in a contest and cause like this, we will smile at the flames, and shake hands with the fagot, and say unto the one, Thou art my sister, and unto the other, Thou art my brother.

Now therefore we pray thee, O king, revoke these thy said ill advised commandments, for they are oppressive to freedom and to thy servants consciences.

Otherwise we do most firmly resolve, that we will have no farther dealings with thy people; and that in the space of sixty days we [65] will not traffick with them for their TEA, their tea cups, their saucers, nor their slop bowls.

Neither shall they with us nor our people, for our iron, our tobacco, our oil, nor our cod fish; what we will make no covenant with them, neither marry nor intermarry.

For what portion have we in Rehoboam, or what inheritance in the grandson of Solomon?

And whereas thou pridest thyself, our raiment will wax old, and we shall go naked and barefooted, knowest thou not, O king, the Lord our God clothed our forefathers in the wilderness, and their garments waxed not old, neither did their feet swell?

For doth not the moon give light, in the absence of the sun, and the stars twinkle when the moon is hid, and the candle shineth when the heavens are black?

Thus, and thus, and more also, did the men of the Congress write unto the king,[27] and moreover they wrote letters unto Thomas sirnamed the Gageite, saying,

Are we not labouring for peace, but when we speak thereof, ye make yourselves ready for battle.

Nevertheless it is thought the king will not hearken unto them, but harden his heart, like unto the heart of Pharaoh, for his eyes are blinded with the pestilential breath of the [66] NORTH wind,[28] so that he cannot see the evil day which is not afar off.

Then shall come to pass, that which was spoken of old by Mordecai, the Benjamite and prophet, saying,

Wo unto the land whose king is a child,[29] whose counsellors are madmen, and whose nobles are tyrants, that devise wicked counsel, for they shall be broken like potters clay.[30]

Wo unto them that draw iniquity with cords of oppression, and sin as with cart ropes,[31] for they shall be afraid of a shadow that passeth by, and the eccho of a toad shall be to them like thunder.

Wo unto the king whose nobles mouths are bridled with a golden bit, and whose governors and rulers persecute the people, for his strength shall decay, his glory tumble in the dust, and his name shall be like unto an old woman's tate.

Wo unto them that decree wicked decrees, and write grievous things, for their hands shall be full, and they shall dip their pens in the gall of bitterness.

Wo unto the king who persecutes his people with sword and with famine, for in the day of desolation the pestilence, like a two edged sword, shall sweep away his host like Pharoah's in the Red sea,[32] or like unto a flood that sweepeth away the pismires in the gutter.

Wo unto the princes of Babel,[33] for they are fools, and the counsel of the king's counsellors are become foolish, for the children of America shall mock them, and shall say, Aha, Babylon is fallen![34] Be wise now therefore, O ye kings, be learned ye that are judges of the earth,[35] kiss the Americans lest they be angry and turn away from ye and curse ye, for blessed are all they that shaketh hands with them in peace.[36]

Now when Jedediah the priest had read all the words of the Congress, and when he had made an end thereof,

He said unto all the people who listened unto him with great attention, for the words of his mouth were sweeter than honey, and the sound of his voice like unto a trumpet, which reached from one end of the land to the other.

Now if thou shalt diligently obey the voice of the Congress, and observe to do all their commandments, which they have commanded thee this day, then shalt thou be set on high above all the nations of the earth.[37]

And blessed shalt thou be in the city, and blessed also in the field.[38]

Blessed shall be thy basket and thy dough.[39]

Blessed shalt thou be when thou comest in, and blessed also when thou goest out.[40]

Blessed shall be thy flocks and thine herds, for they shall bring forth cream in great plen[68]teousness, that thine eyes will wax fat like butter.[41]

Blessed shall be thy shoes, for they shall be soft, made of velvet, and thy feet shall not swell.

Blessed shall be thy toes, for thou shalt have no corns.

Blessed shall be thy chimnies, for they shall not smoke, and with the best of fuel shall thy fire be replenished, it shall burn as clear as the sun at noon day,[42] and thy wife shall hold her peace.

Blessed shall be thy plough, for thine own hands shall guide it, and thine oxen shall speedily walk the furrows, and

Blessed shall he be that blesseth thee.

Then shalt thine enemies that rise against thee, fall before thy face, they shall come out against thee one way, and shall flee before thee seven ways.[43]

And now hearken, O ye innumerable multitude, what I say unto you,

Beware lest any man spoil you through philosophy, vain babbling, jingling of words, sham pretences, pompous speeches, pertinacious double faced scribbling, or letter pressing, and cause ye to stray from the right path.

For behold I say unto you many false prophets, C----ites, and R----ites shall arise, so as to deceive the very elect.[44]

[69] Therefore take heed lest ye be taken in traps and snares, and ye become slaves for life, and thy children after ye, worse than the Ethiopians, or the

Israelites, who were compelled to make brick without straw, or those who are chained for life to tug at the oar.

Now behold Jedediah the priest came down a little way, and Phineas, the son of Eleazar, mounted and stood in his place, and he spake aloud and said, cursed be he that confirmeth not all the words of the law of the Congress, to observe them, and to do them,[45] and all the people said, So be it.

Cursed shalt thou be in the city, and cursed also in the field, and all the people said, So be it.[46]

Cursed shall be thy basket and thy dough, and all the people said, So be it.[47]

Cursed shalt thou be when thou comest in, and cursed also when thou goest out, and all the people said, So be it.[48]

Cursed shall be thy flocks and thine herds, for they shall bring forth skim milk in scarcity,[49] and thy legs shall fall away, like unto a candle that is fried, and all the people said, So be it.

Cursed shall be thy shoes, for they shall be hard, made of the skin of a dromedary, and thou shalt be eternally roaring with the gout, and all the people said, So be it.

[70] Cursed shall be thy toes, for thou shalt have corn by the bushel, and all the people said, So be it.

Cursed shall be thy chimnies, for they shall for ever smoke, and with sodden fuel, rotten stumps and swamp oak, shall thy fire go out; it shall burn like the star Saturn, and the tongue of thy wife shall make an eternal clack, more sonorous and piercing than the tongue of Zantippe, the wife of Socrates, the mother of all scolds, and who kept a scolding school at Athens,[50] and all the people said, So be it.

Cursed be he that putteth his hand to the plough and looketh back, for his oxen shall break their gears, and ramble through the bushes, the briars, and the brambles, and all the people said, So be it.

And cursed shall be he that curseth thee, and all the people lifted up their hands, and fell to the ground, and the whole multitude cried with a loud voice, and said, Like as thou hast spoken, so will we do, and they gave their hands to one another, and answered and said, Amen, Amen, and Amen, so be it.

Notes to the Text

The Geneva Bible and the King James version were the Bibles most commonly available during the eighteenth century. The Geneva Bible, the great Puritan Bible, predominated in the colonies. Its dedication to Queen Elizabeth, exhorting her to show no mercy to Roman Catholics, was appropriate for colonial Puritans seeking freedom from hierarchical domination. In addition, its special features—marginal glosses of particularly difficult texts, especially, in later editions, of Revelation and the Apocrypha—made it singularly useful. The Geneva Bible seems to have been brought to America in 1607, when it was used in the Jamestown colony; and it was brought on the *Mayflower* to Plymouth in 1620.[*] In fact, most of the early New England sermons were based almost exclusively on texts drawn from the Geneva Bible.[†] Because his text concerned the ministry in New England, it would have been fitting that Leacock appropriate the Geneva Bible translation for his *American Chronicles*. Leacock had ready access to the Geneva version: the Cash-Leacock family Bible, now located at the American Philosophical Society, is one of the 160 editions of the Geneva Bible.

In only a few places (e.g., 4.21) did Leacock appropriate the King James version. For instance, Rehoboam's assertion to Thomas the Gageite, "Make their yoke more grievous, my Grandfather corrected them with rods, but I will chastise them with scourges" (2.13) closely resembles 1 Kings 12.11 of the Geneva Bible: "Now where as my father did burden you with a grievous yoke, I will yet make your yoke heavier: my father hath chastised you with rods, but I will correct you with scourges" (typography modernized). The King James version of the text reads: "And now whereas my father did lade you with a heavy yoke, I will add to your yoke: my father hath chastised you with whips, but I will chastise you with scorpions." The Geneva Bible translation is clearly much closer to Leacock's rendering of the text.

---

[*] For a brief background on the Geneva Bible, see P. Marion Simms, *The Bible in America* (New York: Wilson-Erickson, 1936), 75–78, 89–93; and Lloyd E. Berry, intro., *The Geneva Bible: A Facsimile of the 1560 Edition* (Madison: University of Wisconsin Press, 1969), 22. My discussion is drawn from Simms and Berry and from Katherine R. Firth, *The Apocalyptic Tradition in Reformation Britain, 1530–1645* (Oxford: Oxford University Press, 1979), 120–25, and passim.

[†] Berry, *The Geneva Bible*, 22.

Often Leacock used the Geneva Bible verbatim. When the selectmen warn, for example, that "when one churneth milk it bringeth forth butter, and he that wringeth his nose causeth blood to come out, so he that forceth wrath bringeth forth strife" (3.6), their words are nearly an exact transcription of Proverbs 30.33 of the Geneva version (the one change: Leacock substituted the "it" for "he"). The King James version of the same passage differs: "Surely the churning of milk bringeth forth butter, and the wringing of the nose bringeth forth blood: so the forcing of wrath bringeth forth strife." Other comparisons would show that Leacock clearly favors the Geneva Bible in his transcriptions throughout the text.

In the notes that follow, Bible texts are quoted from the Berry facsimile edition of the 1560 Geneva Bible. I have modernized the typography. That is, I have replaced, where necessary, *v* with *u*, *u* with *v*, *i* with *j*, and so forth. And I have replaced tilda marks with the *ns* or *ms* they signify (e.g., "lād" is now "land"). I have not modernized the spelling.

In addition, sources of information in the notes to the text section are identified in abbreviated form there. Complete entries for these sources can be found in the Bibliography section.

Chapter 1

1. great city . . . afar off: London.
2. men of Boston . . . the east: Parliament made the Tea Act law on 10 May 1773, allowing the East India Company to export tea directly to America, so that the Company could undersell smuggled tea and gain a monopoly of the tea trade (taking profits away from the Boston merchant middlemen). When ships first sailed into Boston harbor and met colonial protest, they turned around without unloading the cargo. When Governor Thomas Hutchinson ordered that no ship could leave the harbor without unloading its cargo, the people of Boston and surrounding communities took action. Dressed in Indian headdress and with painted faces, the "redskins" dumped the tea of the *Dartmouth* into Boston harbor on 16 December 1773 (Galvin, 262–65; Jensen, 434–43).
3. Lord . . . wroth: See Matt. 18.34. King George III seems to have believed the Massachusetts reaction to the Tea Act was unjustifiable. Of the Boston Tea Party he wrote to Dartmouth, secretary of colonial affairs, 19 January 1774: "I am hurt that the instigation of bad men hath again drawn the people of Boston to take such unjustifiable steps" (quoted, Christie and Labaree, 182). George III is Rehoboam, 2.11. See note 11, chapter 2.
4. form . . . changed: "Then was Nebuchadnezzar full of rage, and the forme of his visage was changed against Shadrach, Meshach, and Abednego: therefore he charged and commanded that they shulde heate the fornace at once seven times more then it was wonte to be heat" (Dan. 3.19).
5. great Sanhedrim: The Sanhedrin was the great council of the Jewish church and people; it held chief authority in all civil and ecclesiastical cases *(Bible Dict.)*. Leacock refers to the Privy Council, which met on 29 January 1774. News of the Boston Tea Party had reached London on 19 January, via John Hancock's ship *Hayley*. In the 29 January meeting, the cabinet resolved to secure the colonies' dependence on Britain (Jensen, 454).

6. decree: The Boston Port Bill, signed by the King on 31 March 1774. News of the bill reached Boston on 10 May 1774. The Boston Port Bill closed the port to all shipping (effective 1 June), transferred Boston customs activities to Marblehead, and moved the government administration to Salem (Jensen, 454–56, 464; Galvin, 272–75; Patterson, 74).

7. sons of Belial: Biblically, "wicked men." See Deut. 13.33; Judg. 19.22; 1 Sam. 10.27.

8. Mordecai . . . above: Mordecai is Benjamin Franklin. In the Book of Esther, Mordecai saved the life of King Ahasuerus by informing Esther of a plot to kill the king. When Mordecai angered the king's favorite, Haman (analogized in the satire as Lord North, chap. 6), by refusing to reverence him, Haman influenced Ahasuerus to order Mordecai's execution and the destruction of all the Jews. At a banquet for Esther, Haman, and the king, Esther revealed Haman as the enemy of her people, and Ahasuerus ordered Haman hanged on the gallows originally prepared for Mordecai. Mordecai then became second only to the king (*Bible Dict.*). Franklin was Postmaster-General at the time of the Boston Tea Party. At age 68, Franklin had accomplished so much that he was a formidable opponent to the North ministry. Until around July 1773, Franklin pretended that he believed the ministry, not the king, responsible for the adverse measures used against the colonies. In the fall of 1773, however, Franklin attacked both ministry and king in London's *Public Advertiser* by publishing *Rules by Which a Great Empire May Be Reduced to a Small One* and *An Edict by the King of Prussia* (Van Doren, 451ff.).

9. Mordecai . . . ever: Franklin petitioned from August 1773 until January 1774 on behalf of the Massachusetts Assembly for the removal of Governor Thomas Hutchinson and Lieutenant-Governor (and ex-Stamp Distributor) Andrew Oliver. His petition was officially presented on 11 January 1774, in Privy Council. He was there attacked by Solicitor-General Alexander Wedderburn, so he decided to seek further counsel. He presented the petition on 29 January (Van Doren, 456–76).

10. Bernardites: Francis Bernard had been governor of Massachustts, 1760–69. He was relatively powerless against the Massachusetts radicals, and he continually requested military protection in Boston. Bernard was accused by "A True Patriot" (Joseph Warren) in the 29 February 1768 *Boston Gazette* of having misrepresented to the ministry the Massachusetts situation. In April 1769, the publication of some of Bernard's letters to Lord Barrington proved that he had misrepresented the people of Boston. By June, life in Boston became so uncomfortable for Bernard that he readily accepted recall, and he left Boston in July. Bernard's removal left Lieutenant-Governor Thomas Hutchinson in charge (Galvin, 110–80).

11. Hutchinsonians: Thomas Hutchinson became governor of Massachusetts after Francis Bernard's removal from that post in 1769. After his letters to Whately became known, Hutchinson was so unpopular in Boston that he petitioned the ministry for a leave of absence, 26 June 1773. He left Boston in the summer of 1774 and never returned (Bailyn, *Ordeal*, 221–73). See note below.

12. letters . . . hand: The famous "Whately" or "Hutchinson" letters included correspondence from Thomas Hutchinson to Thomas Whately, who had held office under both Grenville and North. In the first publication in Boston by Edes and Gill (1773), the letters to Whately included six from Hutchinson before he had become governor, four from Andrew Oliver before he had become lieutenant-governor, and one letter each from Charles Paxton and Nathaniel Rogers. In addition there was one letter from Robert Auchmuty to Hutchinson (see Thomas R. Adams, no. 96). Calling for the provincial rulers' financial independence from the colony and for possible force to ensure their own safety, the writers emphasized their dislike and distrust of the popular Massachusetts leaders. The letters were transmitted by Franklin (who never revealed how he had obtained

them) to Thomas Cushing in December 1772. Their transmission resulted not only in the Massachusetts Assembly's petition for the removal of Hutchinson and Oliver but also in a bungled duel between William Whately, Whately's brother and executor, and John Temple, a customs officer and friend of Franklin. Whately and Temple blamed each other for the release of the letter packet. When the two agreed upon a second duel, Franklin issued a formal statement of responsibility in *The London Chronicle* of 25 December 1773 (Franklin, *Papers* 19:403–4; 20:513–16; 21:14–17, 48–53; Van Doren, 440–58). See Isa. 3.9.

13. one . . . Wedderburnite: Alexander Wedderburn denounced Franklin in the Privy Council meeting on 29 January, labeling him a thief and a conspirator against the British government (Franklin, *Papers* 20:474n, 540; 21:20–23, 37–68; Van Doren 462–67; *DNB*).

14. Mordecai . . . them: "Then said Paul unto him, God will smite thee, thou whited wall: for thou sittest to judge me according to the Law, and commandest thou me to be smiten contrary to the Law?" (Acts 23.3). Through the counsel of John Dunning, Franklin declined to be examined after Wedderburn's attack, and he quietly left the meeting (Franklin, *Papers* 21:41–42, 68; Van Doren, 466).

15. cried . . . Mordecai: Franklin later wrote to Cushing that not one member of the Privy Council "checked and recalled the orator to the business before them, but on the contrary (a very few excepted) they seemed to enjoy highly the entertainment, and frequently burst out in loud applause" (Franklin, *Papers* 21:92).

16. take . . . post: As indicated by his 15 February letter to Thomas Cushing, Franklin had known of his intended removal as postmaster-general before Wedderburn's cockpit denunciation. He officially learned of his dismissal on 30 January (Franklin, *Papers* 21:90; Van Doren, 463, 476).

17. persecuted . . . more: Although the government frequently opened Franklin's correspondence before Wedderburn's cockpit speech, it systematically opened Franklin's mail after the incident, including letters from his sister, Jane Mecom (Van Doren, 481).

18. Job: Job's patience is proverbial. In Shakespeare's time, Job was evidently viewed as the personification of poverty and patience, as indicated by Falstaff's comment in *2 Henry IV*, "I am as poor as Job, my lord, but not so patient" (1.2.144).

19. Seventh . . . Gageites: The decision to call Hutchinson to England and send Thomas Gage to America as Commanding General of the British Army was made between March and April 1774. Gage arrived in Boston harbor on 13 May (Jensen, 459, 465). Leacock must have known that the recall and replacement took place much earlier than 14 July.

The Boston ministers, led by Charles Chauncy, had refused to read any proclamations of the Governor and Council. When Gage refused to appoint a day of fasting and prayer (because he believed the request was made only to give opportunity for seditious remarks), the ministers themselves proposed that 14 July be observed. On this day, political sermons, some violent in tone, were preached in Boston and New York (Baldwin, 123).

20. Choose . . . Bostonites: Gage left Plymouth on 18 April with three regiments of replacement troops originally destined for Quebec, Halifax, St. Augustine, and New Providence. British Navy ships arrived in Boston harbor almost every day in the latter part of May, and it was quite apparent that the harbor was under seige. Gage evidently had unequivocal permission to employ his troops against disturbances and to punish the perpetrators of the Tea Party (Christie and Labaree, 189; Galvin, 276).

21. spies abroad: Moses sent spies into Canaan. See Num. 13.3, 17, 26; 14.36; Deut. 1.22; Heb. 3.17.

22. rent . . . softly: See 2 Sam. 3.31; Neh. 9.1; Jon. 3.5.

23. 1.18–22: Boston resumed nonimportation measures that had originally been adopted at the time of the Stamp Act in 1765. On 12 May 1774, shortly after news that

the Boston Port Bill had arrived, the Boston Committee of Correspondence called a town meeting. With eight other Committees from nearby towns in attendance, members jointly prepared letters to Committees of Correspondence throughout New England, asking that all exports and imports with Britain and the West Indies be stopped (Jensen, 463–66).

24. Jedediah the scribe: Jedediah is the name given Solomon by the prophet Nathan (2 Sam. 24–25). This is the only place in which Jedediah is called a scribe; beginning with 1.19, he is thereafter called a priest. Jedediah the scribe is perhaps Samuel Adams. Jedediah the priest is most likely Samuel Cooper. See the Introduction.

25. book of the law: The commandments Moses gave the people were to be read every seven years (Deut. 31.10).

26. 1.20: "When all Israel shal come to appeare before the Lord thy God, in the place which he shal chose, thou shalt read this Lawe before all Israel that they may heare it" (Deut. 31.11). The Old South was the scene for the mass assembly in which it was agreed that the tea from the *Dartmouth* should be dumped. The ship's owner had been instructed to demand a pass from Governor Hutchinson so that his ship could depart with the tea. Hutchinson refused to grant a pass, which precipitated patriot action (Labaree, 191–92).

27. understanding . . . commandment: "And of the children of Issachar which were men that had understanding of the times, to knowe what Israel oght to do: the heades of them were two hundreth; and all their brethren were at their commandment" (1 Chron. 12.32).

28. hearkened . . . law: Support for the nonimportation measures spread through the colonies, though most colonies would not agree to the Solemn League and Covenant (see next note).

29. solemn league and covenant: At a town meeting 30 May 1774, the Boston Committee of Correspondence was directed to prepare a formal document for nonimportation and nonconsumption. By 2 June, Joseph Warren had been appointed chair of the Committee to draft the document, which was called the Solemn League and Covenant. (The name reflected its biblical and Cromwellian precedent. Cromwell's compact of the same name, aimed at Charles I, abolished episcopacy, settled liturgy, and established canons.) At a town meeting in Boston on 27 June, the turnout of merchants (who wished to see the Boston Committee and its Covenant censured) was so large that the meeting had to move to the Old South, where it was voted that the letters of the Committee and the Solemn League be read aloud (Jensen, 468–70; Matthews, "Solemn League"). Frustrated, the merchants wrote an address to Thomas Hutchinson, insisting upon their faith in his service. The protesters also published their protest and their names on at least two occasions in the *Massachusetts Gazette*, 2 June and 7 June (Frothingham; Deane; Patterson, 74–79).

30. And . . . land: The merchant factions in the cities opposed nonimportation for obvious financial reasons; the colonists nonetheless sent provisions to Boston (Jensen, 468–70; Christie and Labaree, 201).

31. ready . . . land: "Moreover they that were nere them until Issachar, and Zebulun, and Naphtali broght bread upon asses, and on camels, and on mules, and on oxen, even meat, floure, figges, & reisins, and wine & oyle, & beves and shepe abundantly: for there was joye in Israel" (1 Chron. 12.40).

32. proclamation . . . piety: Gage made a "Proclamation for the Encouragement of Piety and Virtue" and issued it in July 1774. The proclamation is reproduced in Appendix C. See chapter 4.

33. Obadiah: The prophet of the Book of Obadiah denounces Judah's traditional enemies and prophesies the deeds and dreams that will be brought to fruition in the reign of the Lord on Zion (*Bible Dict.*). Obadiah is probably John Hancock. See the Introduction.

34. Ezekiel: Ezekiel was the sixth major prophet of the Exilic period. His dual role as prophet-priest makes Ezekiel's position unique among Old Testament personages. His position as watchman over the exiles is defined in terms of a pastor's concern for the spiritual welfare of the flock (*Bible Dict.*). I am unable to identify the person fictionalized as Ezekiel.

35. Jonathan . . . Ebenezer: Jonathan was the son of Saul who never succeeded to the throne of Israel. He bore no resentment to David when David ascended the throne; in fact, their friendship is one of the greatest in biblical history (*Bible Dict.*). The name *Jonathan* was used during the Revolutionary War, according to Albert C. Matthews, "as a mildly derisive epithet, by the Loyalists, and applied by them to those who espoused the American cause." Later in the century, the Americans took it up themselves and used it to describe a country bumpkin. Finally, the name came into popular use as a name for any American (Matthews, "Brother Jonathan," 108–12).

36. defileth . . . day: Prior to the Revolution, British soldiers harassed the colonists by marching and playing such tunes as "Yankee Doodle" during church services. In his letter of 12 September 1774, John Andrews reported that officers and soldiers "in service time in particular, in traversing the streets and by-ways, . . . tamper with the children, to get out of them where the cannon were hid." And his letter of 18 March 1774 described the disturbances on religious holidays: "Thursday [16 March] was observ'd here as a general fast. An officer, with men from the 4th regiment in Barracks at West Boston, erected a couple of tents just at the back of Harvard's meeting and conducted a parcell of fifes and drums there, which play'd and beat Yanky Doodle the whole forenoon service time, to the great interruption of the congregation" (Andrews, 46, 87; Lemay, "Yankee Doodle"). See note 34, chapter 2.

37. send . . . us: The Committees of Correspondence of various surrounding towns shared declarations and information during the Boston seige (Jensen, 471–79).

38. hewers . . . water: The Gibeonites, who beguiled Joshua by saying they had come from afar, were made into hewers of wood and drawers of water as punishment (Josh. 9.20–27).

39. Send . . . brethren: The Boston patriots had long feared that intercolonial contention might arise from a Continental Congress. They finally agreed to meet and conducted a secret meeting on 17 June 1774 to elect five delegates to send to Philadelphia. John and Samuel Adams, Thomas Cushing, Robert Treat Paine, and James Bowdoin were elected. Bowdoin could not attend the Congress (Jensen, 469).

40. And . . . Month: The delegates from the various states met at a tavern on Monday, 5 September, and chose to meet at Carpenters Hall (rather than at the State House offered by Joseph Galloway). On 6 September, they resolved to appoint a committee to state the rights of the colonies in general. By Wednesday, 7 September, they were debating the theoretical foundation of American rights (Jensen, 490–93).

41. 1.32–34: On Tuesday, 6 September, a rumor arrived in Philadelphia that the British soldiers had killed six Americans while seizing powder near Boston and that the British fleet had bombarded Boston for a whole night. Later that day, Congress learned the tale was false. The false report had begun when, early in the morning on 1 September, Gage's troops seized some powder stored by Massachusetts farmers near Cambridge. When a crowd gathered, demanding the resignation of the Mandamus Councilors whom Gage had appointed after the arrival of the Massachusetts Government Act in early August, the Boston Committee of Correspondence, under the leadership of Joseph Warren, helped head off violence (Jensen, 492, 535–37). The *Boston Evening-Post* of 5 September ran a long account of the powder seizure and patriot response. See Appendix C for the account.

42. captives . . . laws: Nebuchadnezzar made the Jews captive at Babylon, the metropolis of Chaldea, on the site of the tower of Babel (2 Kings 25; 2 Chron. 36; Jer. 39, 52).

43. Aminadab: Biblically, Amminadab, Aminadab, or Aminadib refers to one of two men: 1) the ancestral head of a family or clan of Judah; 2) the name of one or more Levites, descendants of Kohath (*Bible Dict.*). Aminadab probably represents William Cooper. See the Introduction.

44. Jeremiah: Many Jeremiahs appear in the Bible. This Jeremiah is probably one of the three major prophets who attacked the apostasy of the people, the immoralities of life, the self-deception of superficial reformers, and dangerous alliances. Combative by nature, he aimed his attacks at temple priests, false prophets, vindictive rulers, and military authorities (*Bible Dict.*). Jeremiah is probably the Reverend Dr. Charles Chauncy. See the Introduction.

45. New Canaan: The subjugation of Canaan and its inhabitants was the goal of Israel's conquest. Jerusalem did not fall to Israel until the reign of David.

46. desolate . . . widow: "And she that is a widowe in dede, and left alone, trusteth in God, & continueth in supplications and prayers night and day" (1 Tim. 5.5). The fragile woman in the wilderness, especially one beset by the malignant red dragon, was one of the most common images of America used in sermons (Hatch, 60–61).

47. She . . . Askalon: "O noble Israel, he is slaine upon thy hie places: how are the mighty overthrowen? Tel it not in Gath, nor publish it in the stretes of Ashkelon, lest the daughters of the Philistims rejoyce, lest the daughters of the uncircumcised triumphe" (2 Sam. 1.19–20).

48. 1.38: "And David said to all the Congregation of Israel, If it seme good to you, and that it procedeth of the Lord our God, we wil send to and fro unto our brethren, that are left in all the land of Israel (for with them are the Priests and Levites in the cities and their suburbes) that they may assembly them selves unto us" (1 Chron. 13.2). See also Gen. 24.50.

49. And . . . people: "And all the Congregation answered, Let us do so: for the thing semed good in the eyes of all the people" (1 Chron. 13.4).

50. Now . . . arise: The powder scare spread rapidly through the back country. In his letter of 2 September, John Andrews wrote about this alarm and the response it received:

> [A] report prevail'd through the country (by reason of the seizure of the powder yesterday) that y^e. same game had been play'd here, and y^e. inhabitants disarm'd has rais'd such a spirit as will require the utmost prudence to allay; for they are in arms at all quarters, being determin'd to see us redress'd. At eight o'clock this morning there were about three thousand under their regular leaders at Cambridge common, and continually increasing; had left their arms at a little distance, when Judge Lee and Danforth waited upon 'em, and gave them the fullest assurances that they had resigned their seats . . . . Lieutenant Governor Oliver is come to town and Brattle [who had ordered the seizure] is gone to the Castle, which I believe is the only place of safety for him in the province. Four or five expresses have come down to Charlestown and here, to acquaint us, that between Sudbury and this, above ten thousand men are in arms and are continually coming down from the country back: that their determination is to collect about forty or fifty thousand by night (which they are sure of accomplishing) when they intend to fling in about fifteen thousand by way of the Neck, and as many more over the ferry. . . . (Andrews 38–39) .

On 25 September, Joseph Read of Philadelphia wrote to Dartmouth that the fury over the powder scare was so great that "thousands would have gone at their own expense, to have joined in the revenge. It was difficult to make them doubt the intelligence [that blood had been shed], or delay setting out." If the news had been true, he said, an army of 40,000 men, well-armed with everything except cannon, would have marched to Boston (quoted in Jensen, 536–37). See notes 41 above and 56 below.

51. that . . . Louisburgites: The colonists captured Louisburg from the French in 1745. They were justly proud of this achievement, for, as S. Foster Damon has written,

"[u]nlike the recapture of this French stronghold in 1758, the expedition of 1745 was undertaken by locally recruited New England troops and it had succeeded against all likelihood" (2). See Lemay, "Yankee Doodle."

52. be . . . dismayed: "And the Lord him selfe doeth go before thee: he willbe with thee: he wil not fayle thee, nether forsake thee: feare not therefore, nor be discomforted" (Deut. 31.8).

53. the Lord . . . Lord: "And he said, Hearken ye, all Judah, & ye inhabitants of Jerusalem, and thou, King Jehoshaphat: thus saith the Lord unto you, Feare not, nether be afraied for this great multitude: for the battel is not yours, but Gods" (2 Chron. 20.15). See also 1 Sam. 18.17, 25.28.

54. Caleb: Caleb was one of twelve spies sent out with Joshua to survey the strength of Canaan (Num. 13, 14). The son of Jephunneh the Kenizzite, he was believed certain to see the Promised Land because he had "constantly followed the Lord" (Deut. 1.36). Caleb was the only one of the spies who thought Israel strong enough to occupy the land (Num. 13.30). Caleb probably represents Joseph Warren. See the Introduction. See notes 41 and 50 above, and note 56 below.

55. The . . . thousands: "And David counseled with the captaines of thousands & of hundreths, & with all the governours" (1 Chron. 13.1).

56. 1.45: The first reaction to the powder scare outside Boston came from the Massachusetts back country. For instance, the rumor reached Worcester that afternoon, and perhaps 6,000 men from Worcester county started east before the story was contradicted. Benjamin Church informed John Adams in a letter dated 4 September 1774 that about 20,000 men from the western towns started to march on Boston and were persuaded only with great difficulty to turn back (Jensen, 536; Brown, 347–48). The valley of Ephraim was rugged, olive-clad terrain set in the central range of Palestine. It was the scene of the fierce battle between David and Absalom (2 Sam. 18.6). See notes 41 and 50 above.

57. 1.46–54: This section is reminiscent of 1 Chron. 10–12.

58. 1.46: "These also are they that came to David to Ziklag, while he was yet kept close, because of Saul the sonne of Kish: and they were among the valiant and helpers of the battel"; "And these are the nombers of the captaines that were armed to battel, & came to David to Hebron to turne the kingdome of Saul to him, according to the worde of the Lord"; "These were the sonnes of Gad, captaines of the hoste: one of the least colde resist an hundreth, and the greatest a thousand"; "And of the Gadites there separated them selves some unto David into the holde of the wilderness, valiant men of warre, and men of armes, & apt for battel, which colde handle a speare and shield, and their faces were like the faces of lyons, and were like the roes in the mountains in swiftenes" (respectively, 1 Chron. 12.1, 23, 14, 8).

59. Colossus at Rhodes: A bronze of Apollo, one of the seven wonders of the ancient world, which fell to the ground in an eqarthquake in 224 B.C.

60. Israel: Israel is the name given to Jacob by an angel at the Jabbok ford on the eve of his reunion with his brother and also given by God at Bethel (Gen. 32.28; 35.10). The Genesis accounts of the activities of Jacob and his sons make this Patriarch the direct ancestor of the Hebrew nation. I am unable to identify the person fictionalized as Israel.

61. Jonathan: See note 35 above.

62. that . . . breadth: "Of all this people were seven hundreth chosen men, being left handed: all these colde sling stones at an heere breadth, and not faile" (Judg. 20.16).

63. Nathan: Six Nathans are in the Bible, and four of them might be the *Nathan* Leacock means: 1) the son of David, born in Jerusalem, who appears in Luke's genealogy of Jesus (3.31); 2) a prophet and chaplain at the court of David; 3) the father of Igal, an officer of David's; 4) a man who returned from Exile with Ezra and was appointed to

secure ministers for the house of God (*Bible Dict.*). I am unable to identify the person fictionalized as Nathan.

64. Eleazer: This is the name of at least eleven men in the Bible. The most prominent Eleazer was the third son of Aaron, who became chief of the Levites and the overseer of the sanctuary custodians. He succeeded Aaron as high priest, an office he held during the remainder of Moses's life and under Joshua's leadership (*Bible Dict.*). I am unable to identify the person fictionalized as Eleazer.

65. Reuben: Reuben is the eldest of the twelve sons of Jacob in the Bible. Jacob laments his instability. Reuben suggested casting Joseph into the pit rather than killing him (as his brothers had wished to do). In the era of Judges, Reuben's tribe proved indifferent to the crisis of Israel and the Canaanites, preferring to remain with their flocks while their brothers fought against the common foe (*Bible Dict.*). I am unable to identify the person fictionalized as Reuben.

66. Hezekiah: This is the name of the fourteenth King of Judah, the son and successor of Ahaz. He resorted to prayer when the Assyrian army came to reduce Jerusalem, and the Assyrians were defeated (*Bible Dict.*). I am unable to identify the person fictionalized as Hezekiah.

67. Goliah of Gath: Goliath was the nine-foot Philistine giant whose slaying by David carried religious connotations (*Bible Dict.*).

68. Pelatiah: This use of the name probably refers to the name of a family that sealed the Covenant (Neh. 10.22). I am unable to identify the person fictionalized as Pelatiah.

69. Zedekiah: Probably refers to the last King of Judah. During the fourth year of his reign, he had trouble with Nebuchadnezzar, who sent the Chaldeans to beseige the city, which capitulated six years later. Zedekiah was fettered and carried to Babylon and imprisoned until his death (*Bible Dict.*). I am unable to identify the person fictionalized as Zedekiah.

70. Sampson: Folk tales about Samson abound. One of the mosts renowned Hebrew judges, he was unique in that his birth and manner of life were foretold. Supernaturally endowed, he killed a lion, thirty Philistines, and one thousand men. He broke the strongest bonds, carried off the gates of Gaza, and pulled down the Temple of Dagon (*Bible Dict.*).

71. hard . . . knot: Mencken pointed out that *pine knot* "belonged to the colonial period" (115). The earliest figurative use in expressing the hardness and toughness of pine has been noted as 1812, when James Kirke Paulding used it in his comic account of the settlement, growth, and revolt of the American colonies, *The Diverting History of John Bull and Brother Jonathan* (*DAE; DA; Dict. of Am. Prov.*).

72. Zechariah: Twenty-nine men have this name in the Bible. The reference here is probably to the minor prophet who carried on, primarily through the use of apocalyptic visions and visions of Christ, an urgent appeal to rebuild the Temple (*Bible Dict.*). I am unable to identify the person fictionalized as Zechariah.

73. Joshua: Four Joshuas appear in the Bible. This is probably the Joshua mentioned in Exodus 17, who was selected by Moses to rout the Amalkites, whom he had defeated in a great victory in Sinai, and who was chosen to succeed Moses as the leader from Egypt to Canaan. The primary purpose of the Book of Joshua is homiletic, to teach God's will for Israel and to tell of the ultimate victory for the nation (*Bible Dict.*). I am unable to identify the person fictionalized as Joshua.

74. astonied: Astonished—Geneva Bible translation—as in Ezra 9.3; Job 17.8; Dan. 3.24, 4.19.

75. while . . . flee: By eight o'clock on the morning of 1 September, between 3,000 and 4,000 men had gathered in Cambridge, after the powder had been seized. General William Brattle, who had advised Gage to seize the powder, fled to Boston from

Cambridge. Lieutenant-Governor Thomas Oliver urged Gage to keep his troops in Boston to head off violence (Jensen, 536).

Chapter 2

1. Judas the parasite: Judas, the betrayer of Christ, is Thomas Hutchinson, who set sail for London in July 1774, after Gage had arrived in May.

2. 23.2–3: "So they broght up an evil reporte of the land which they had searched for the children of Israel, saying, The land which we have gone through to search it out, is a land that eateth up the inhabitants thereof: for all the people that we sawe in it, are men of great stature. For there we sawe gyantes, the sonnes of Anak, which come of the gyantes, so that we semed in our sight like greshoppers: and so we were in their sight" (Num. 13.33–34).

3. set . . . tokens: "That we may rejoyce in thy salvation, and set up the banner in the Name of our God, when the Lord shal performe all thy petitions" (Ps. 20.5).

4. thy . . . strait: "And David said unto Gad, I am in a wonderful straite: let us fall now into the hand of the Lord, (for his mercies are great) and let me not fall into the hand of man" (2 Sam. 24.14).

5. all . . . Egypt: The ten plagues of Egypt formed part of the miracles in the Old Testament. They consisted of: water made into blood, frogs, lice, flies, murrain, boils and blains, thunder and hail, locusts, darkness, and the slaying of the firstborn (Bible Dict.).

6. all . . . resigned: By the summer of 1774, popular pressure forced many of the Mandamus Council members to resign or seek the protection of the British troops in Boston. Only fifteen of the original thirty-six appointees to the Mandamus Council of 1774 remained by the end of September. The patriot reaction to the powder scare caused many of these resignations by 2 September (Brown, 276–77, 340–43). See notes 41, 50, and 56, chapter 1.

7. Job's comforters: Job's comforters attempted to sympathize with him in his grief, but they said that he had brought his problems upon himself, which worsened his sorrow (Job 16).

8. venemous . . . ears: "Their poison is even like the poison of a serpent: like the deafe adder that stoppeth his eare" (Ps. 58.4).

9. bye-word: "And thou shalt be a wonder, a proverbe & a comune talke among all people, whether the Lord shal cary thee" (Deut. 28.37).

10. spirit . . . Devil: See chapter 4.39ff.

11. Rehoboam: Rehoboam was the son of Solomon. When all Israel came to see his coronation, Rehoboam learned of his subjects' grievances over the forced labor and excessive taxation that had supported his father's reign. Rejecting the advice of elder counsel to conciliate the people, Rehoboam followed the advice of younger peers and spoke roughly to his subjects. His threats precipitated the revolt of his northern and eastern subjects, and Rehoboam had to flee to Jerusalem for safety. The apostasies characteristic of Rehoboam's reign include idolatry, illicit rites, false worship, and sodomy (Bible Dict.).

12. resolves: Many counties and towns developed their own resolves in response to the Coercive Acts. The most famous came from the Suffolk Convention in early September 1774. The Suffolk Resolves reflected many of the conflicting sentiments of Americans in general. Cautious in acknowledging George III the rightful sovereign, Suffolk was radical in calling for a complete boycott of the courts of law and for resistance to all officials who might try to execute acts contrary to the provincial charter. Suffolk demanded the resignations of all Mandamus Council members before 20 September, and it called for nonimportation, the encouragement of home manufactures, military training under

officers with "sufficient capacity for that purpose," and a Provincial Congress to meet in Concord in October. Acknowledging that the people should act only on their defense, Suffolk warned that if popular leaders were arrested, "every servant of tyrannical and unconstitutional government should be likewise arrested." The Suffolk Convention appointed a committee to inform Gage of the country's alarm at the fortifications around Boston and sent Paul Revere to hand deliver a copy of the Resolves to the Continental Congress then convening in Philadelphia (Patterson, 97–98; *Prov. Jnls.*, 601–9).

Within the first two weeks of their assembly, the First Continental Congress endorsed the Suffolk Resolves. They then accepted a series of resolutions generally known as the Declaration of Colonial Rights and Grievances. Among these was John Adams's clause asserting the colonial right to self-government in matters of taxation and internal law. The Declaration asserted that only with colonial consent could Parliament regulate colonial commerce to Britain's advantage, provided it made no attempt to raise revenues by such action. Moreover, the Declaration ruled that all existing acts of Parliament that taxed the colonies infringed on colonial rights. Infringements, also, it said, were the Coercive Acts, the Quebec Act, and several other laws, all of which the Declaration called upon Parliament to repeal.

The demands established, the delegates agreed to ban all importations from Britain and Ireland after 1 December 1774. And they resolved that unless American grievances were redressed by 10 September 1775, exports from America to Britain, Ireland, and the West Indies would discontinue. This plan for economic retaliation known as the Continental Association allowed groups of patriots in each town or county to intervene in the private affairs of all citizens. After having adopted addresses to the King and British people, the First Continental Congress adjourned in late October, providing for another Congress to be convened in May 1775, unless colonial grievances were redressed (Patterson, 97–98; *Prov. Jnls.*, 601–9; Lebaree, 198–99). See Thomas the Gageite's lament, 2.2ff., and the "resolutions" of chapter 6. See note 29, chapter 1.

13. But . . . swine: The legion of devils cast away by God's power enter into a herd of swine, which run into the sea and choke to death (Matt. 8.32; Mark 5.13; Luke 8.33).

14. make . . . grievous: "Thy father made our yoke grievous: now therefore make thou the grievous servitude of thy father, and his sore yoke which he put upon us, lighter, & we wil serve thee" (1 Kings 12.4).

15. Grandfather . . . scourges: "Now where as my father did burden you with a grievous yoke, I wil yet make your yoke heavier: my father hathe chastised you with rods, but I wil correct you with scourges" (1 Kings 12.11).

16. portion . . . Quebeckites: The Quebec Act followed the Coercive Acts. It added to the province of Quebec much western territory claimed by several of the colonies; continued the kind of loyalist, unrepresentative government in Quebec that had prevailed under the French; and afforded complete religious toleration to the overwhelmingly Catholic population there. The Quebec Act received the royal assent on 22 June 1774 (Christie and Labaree, 193–96).

17. OCCUNNEOCOGEECOCOCACHEECACHEECADUNGO: The cult of the Indian was reaching its pitch by the end of the eighteenth century in America. Stories about great Indian chiefs became widespread. Leacock knew well the stories about one chief of the Delawares, Tamanend, who was the namesake of a Philadelphia group, the Society of the Sons of Saint Tammany. This social organization, to which Leacock belonged, was an offshoot of the Philadelphia Sons of Liberty. The first meeting of The Society of the Sons of Saint Tammany is recorded in the *Pennsylvania Chronicle*, 4 May 1772. Leacock wrote a group song, "The First of MAY, A NEW SONG, in praise of St. Tammany," which appeared in the *Pennsylvania Evening Post*, Tuesday, 30 April 1776, and in his play, *The Fall of British Tyranny*. Tammany had long been known in Pennsylvania for his friendly services to the first settlers (Cabeen).

The Boston Tea Party was one of a number of noteworthy "Indian" acts. John Adams's diary entry for Tuesday, 8 March 1774, noted the essential facts of a similar incident: "Last Night 28 Chests and an half of Tea were drowned" (2:91). The *Boston Gazette* for 14 March reported that the "drowning" had occurred on orders of "His Majesty OK-NOOKORTUNKOGOG King of the Narraganset Tribe of Indians," whose tribesmen "are now returned to Naragansett to make Report of their doings to his Majesty, who we hear is determined to honour them with Commissions for the Peace."

18. when . . . them: Perhaps an allusion to the French and Indian War, the most noted battle of which took place at Fort Duquesne in the Ohio Valley on 9 July 1755, when a French and Indian force overcame the British army led by General Braddock (Jensen, 4). See note 20 below.

19. Fret . . . herb: "Freate not thy self because of the wicked men, nether be envious for the evil doers. For they shal soone be cut downe like grasse, and shal wither as the grene herbe" (Ps. 37.1–2).

20. one . . . flight: "How shulde one chase a thousand, and two put ten thousand to flight, except their strong God had solde them, & the Lord had shut them up?" (Deut. 32.30). Braddock and the English greatly outnumbered the French and Indians who defeated them.

21. free . . . remain: Part of the refrain of the popular "Liberty Song":

> In freedom we're born, and in freedom we'll live;
> Our purses are ready,
> Steady, Friends, Steady,
> Not as *slaves*, but as *freemen* our money we'll give.

Written by John Dickinson and Arthur Lee, the "Liberty Song" was published first in the *Boston Gazette*, 18 July 1768, as *A Song Now Much in Vogue in North America*. Dickinson had sent the song to James Otis (Moore, 38–42).

22. 2.21: "Why do the heathen rage, & the people murmur in vaine" (Ps. 2.1).

23. 2.22: "The Kings of the earth band them selves, and the princes are assembled together against the Lord, and against Christ" (Ps. 2.2).

24. 2.23: "Let us breake their bands, and cast their cords from us" (Ps. 2.3). The Provincial Congress held in October 1774, after Gage had dissolved the General Court, received many of the same delegates who would have attended the General Court meeting in Salem. Each town sent its own instructions. Worcester, first among the counties to dispense altogether with the traditional vote of allegiance to George III, was most radical. The Worcester delegates declared that if all wrongs had not been redressed and all charter rights restored (they declared the Charter of 1629 had been wrongfully wrested from the colony) by the day the Provincial Congress met, the representatives were to consider the people of Massachusetts in a state of nature, absolved from all charter obligations to Britain (Brown, 352–53; Patterson, 96).

25. Liberty Tree: According to Massachusetts lore, a large oak planted in Boston common in 1646, three years before the execution of Charles I, was the liberty tree. The image of a tree of liberty became a popular symbol for American patriots, and "liberty" trees sprang up throughout the colonies as resistance increased (Hay; Schlesinger, "Liberty Tree").

26. NORTH: Frederick North (1732–92), an agent for George III, dominated the ministry and was probably the closest counselor to the King. Against protests of Fox and Burke, he pursued the ruinous policy of suppression leading to the revolt and loss of the American colonies. North introduced the Boston Port Bill and the Massachusetts Government Act in March 1774 (*DNB*).

27. BUTE: John Stuart, third Earl of Bute (1713–92), the Scottish favorite of George

III, was descended from one of the natural sons of the Stuart kings. As a Privy Councilor and Groom of the Stole, Bute promoted to George III Bolingbroke's doctrine of absolute monarchy. His vote against the repeal of the Stamp Act and his machinations against George III's other ministers made the colonists believe Bute one of their most inimical opponents (*DNB*). Popular opinion was that Bute wished to see a Stuart back on the throne in order to bring his own family back to social and financial prominence. Leacock propagandizes against Bute in *The Fall of British Tyranny*.

28. MANSFIELD: William Murray, first Earl of Mansfield (1705–93), called by Macaulay "the father of modern toryism," favored a policy of coercion with regard to the American colonies. He is credited with having been the author of the Quebec Act, and he fostered the Coercive Acts as they went through Parliament (*DNB*).

29. 2.27–28: "On the morowe as they went on their jorney, and drewe nere unto the citie, Peter went up upon the house to pray, about the sixt houre. Then waxed he an hungred, and wolde have eaten: but while they made some thing readie, he fel into a trance. And he sawe heaven opened, and a certeine vessel come downe unto him, as it had bene a great shete, knit at the foure corners, and was let downe to earth. Wherein were all maner of foure foted beastes of the earth, and wilde beastes, and creping things, and foules of the heaven" (Acts 10.9–12).

30. 2.32: Reminiscent of Dan. 7.

31. waited . . . event: "But if we hope for that we se not, we do with pacience abide for it" (Rom. 8.25).

32. Two . . . broken: "And if one overcome him, two shal stande against him: and a threfolde coard is not easely broken" (Eccles. 4.12).

33. while . . . parade: The people of Boston received abuse on religious, social, and political grounds. In a letter dated 1 August 1774, John Andrews described the antics of some officers who "committed all manner of enormous indecencies, by exposing their anteriors, as well as their posteriors, at the open windows and doors, to the full view of the people, either men or women, that happened to pass by . . ." (*Letters*, 20–21). Andrews remarked also upon the physical abuse and affronts women suffered, even when their husbands were at home (32), and the verbal and physical insults thrust upon the townspeople as they walked in the streets (21, 51–52, 68). See note 36, Chapter 1.

34. Yankeys: By 1774, the term was used not only for natives of New England but for Americans in general. The English used *Yankee* to deride the Americans as ignorant, barbaric yokels. The Americans came to mock the English derision by posturing themselves as yokels, thus duping the English and having the last laugh. During the Revolution and after, the patriots enjoyed mocking the English by playing the tune "Yankee Doodle" and calling themselves *Yankees* (Lemay, "Yankee Doodle"). See note 36, chapter 1.

35. good . . . unity: "Beholde how good and how comelie a thing it is, brethren to dwell even together in unity (Ps. 133.1).

36. Only . . . afraid: "Plucke up your hearts therefore, and be strong: dread not, nor be afrayd of them: for the Lord thy God, him selfe doeth go with thee: he wil not fayle thee, nor forsake thee" (Deut. 31.6). Exhortations like this from Deuteronomy were commonly used in patriot sermons. Baldwin has stated that "in the months before the battle of Lexington, minister after minister, as if in preparation for the coming struggle, called the men to be of stout heart and good courage, ready to wield the sword of the Lord" (126).

37. for . . . them: "For they are a nacion voyde of counsel, nether is there anie understanding in them" (Deut. 32.28).

38. They . . . inventions: "And I am this day weake and newly anointed King: and these men the sonnes of Zeruiah be to hard for me: the Lord reward the doer of evil according to his wickednes" (2 Sam. 3.39).

39. they . . . hands: "For many nacions, and great Kings shal even serve them selves of

them: thus wil I recompence them according to their dedes, and according to the workes of their owne hands" (Jer. 25.14).

40. 2.45–48: Instead of sending his troops into the outlying areas in September and October 1774, Gage decided to fortify the narrow neck of the peninsula on which Boston was built at the time (Brown, 349).

41. builded . . . about: "He shal slaie with the sworde thy daughters in the field, and he shal make a forte against thee, and cast a mount against thee, and lift up the buckler against thee. He shal set engines of warre before him against thy walles, and with his weapons breake downe thy towres" (Ezek. 25.8–9).

42. ships . . . enter: Boston merchants used the ports of Salem and Marblehead during the seige.

43. their God . . . judges: "For their god is not as our God, even our enemies being judges" (Deut. 32.31). Unrest about Boston's plight extended into the back country. Rural extremists wanted Boston sacrificed to American liberty, and they demanded that patriotic Bostonians leave their homes at once. Moderates in Boston disliked the idea of leaving their quarters available to the British regulars, but some agreed with rural thinking (Patterson, 112).

44. Eliphalet: One or possibly two sons of David and one of David's mighty men, along with three other men, were named Eliphalet in the Bible. If Jedediah the priest is Samuel Cooper, then Eliphalet refers to his father, Reverend William Cooper (1694–1743).

45. Ehud . . . Gera: Ehud was a left-handed Benjamite who killed the Eglon King Moab and 10,000 Moabites and became a judge of Israel (*Bible Dict.*).

46. Phineas . . . Eleazer: Phinehas, the son of Eleazer, inherited the land of Ephraim. As successor to his father in the high priesthood, Phinehas rose to prominence in the narrative of the Chronicles. In one incident, he killed an Israelite who, by bringing a Midianite woman into the camp, was responsible for tempting the Hebrews to follow her form of worship (*Bible Dict.*). Phineas is Israel Putnam. John Andrews's letter dated 6 September 1774, written just after the powder scare, noted: "Its allowed, by the best calculations, that at least a hundred thousand men were equipt with arms, and moving towards us from different parts of the country. The *celebrated* Colonel Putnam was at the head of fifteen thousand, and its said that five and twenty thousand more were in a body a day's march behind him" (*Letters*, 42). See the Introduction.

47. Othniel: Othniel was a man of Judah (a younger brother or half-brother to Caleb), whose story is typical of the rise to leadership of the oppressed clans on whom God poured His grace. The writer of Deuteronomy uses the story of Othniel to illustrate the charismatic cycle of Israel's history before the Monarchy (*Bible Dict.*). If Caleb is Joseph Warren, then Othniel is Joseph's younger brother, John. See the Introduction.

48. Select men . . . another: See Mark 9.39. Selectmen were the leading officials in each town (Brown, 61–99).

Chapter 3

1. 3.6: "When one churneth milke, he bringeth forthe butter: and he that wringeth his nose causeth blood to come out: so he that forceth wrath, bringeth forthe strife" (Prov. 30.33).

2. If . . . mouth: "If thou hast bene foolish in lifting thy self up, and if thou hast thoght wickedly, lay thine hand upon thy mouth" (Prov. 30.32).

3. A . . . honour: "A litle citie and fewe men in it, and a great King came against it, and compassed it about, and buylded fortes against it. And there was founde therein a poore and wise man, and he delivered the citie by his wisdom: but none remembred this

poore man. Then said I, Better is wisdome then strength: yet the wisdome of poore men is despised, and his wordes are not heard" (Eccles. 9.14–16).

4. *Honour's . . . good:* Evidently, this is Leacock's verse.

5. Take . . . viols: "Take thou away from me the multitude of thy songs (for I wil not heare the melodie of thy violes)" (Amos 5.23).

6. Tarshish: *Tarshish* is used several times in the Old Testament in reference to ships and ports. Tarshish might originally have been a city that developed a seagoing trade in minerals (*Bible Dict.*).

7. Forty . . . Zin: See Num. 14.33; Ps. 95.10.

8. 3.17–20: "For the Lord thy God bringeth thee into a good land, a land in which are rivers and fountaines, & depthes that spring out of valeis and mountaines: A land of wheat and barley, and of vineyards, and figtrees, & pomegranates: a land of oyle olive and honey: A land wherein thou shalt eat bread without scarcetie, nether shalt thou lack anie thing therein: a land whose stones are yron, & out of whose mountains thou shalt digge brass" (Deut. 8.7–9).

9. Then . . . thou: "Where the worde of the King is, there is power, and who shal say unto him, What doest thou?" (Eccles. 8.4).

10. 3.22: "Because sentence against an evil worke is not executed spedely, therefore the heart of the children of men is fully set in them to do evil" (Eccles. 8.11).

11. better to trust . . . princes: "It is better to trust in the Lord, then to have confidence in princes" (Ps. 118.9).

12. 3.25: "From the which things some have erred, and have turned unto vaine jangling. They wolde be doctours of the Law, and yet understand not what they speake, nether whereof they affirme"; "He is pufte up and knoweth nothing, but doteth about questions and strife of wordes, whereof cometh envie, strife, railings, evil surmisings, vaine disputations of men of corrupt mindes, and destitute of the trueth, which thinke that gaine is godlines: from suche separate thy self" (1 Tim. 1.6–7; 6.4–5).

13. 3.26: "And as Jannes and Jambres with stoode Moses, so do these also resiste the trueth, men of corrupte mindes, reprobate concerning the faith. But they shal prevaile no longer: for their madnes shalbe evident unto all men, as theirs also was" (2 Tim. 3.8–9). Jannes and Jambres were magicians of Egypt.

14. Phineas: See note 46, chapter 2.

15. face . . . ruddy: "And he sent, and broght him in: and he was ruddie, and of a good countinance, & comelie visage. And the Lord said, Arise, & anoint him: for this is he" (1 Sam. 16.12).

16. countenance . . . noonday: "And he had in his right hand seven starres: and out of his mouth went a sharpe two edged sworde: & his face shone as the sunne shineth in his strength" (Rev. 1.16).

17. sons . . . Anak: Ahiman, Sheshai, and Talmai were the sons of Anak, descended from a race of giants (Num. 13.22).

18. captain . . . Louisbourgh: See l.40 and note 51, chapter 1.

19. 3.30: "The King is not saved by the multitude of an hoste, nether is the mightie man delivered by great strength" (Ps. 33.16).

20. wicked . . . neck: "I said unto the foolish, Be not so foolish, and to the wicked, Lift not up the horne. Lift not up your horne on high, nether speake with a stiffe necke" (Ps. 75.4–5).

21. lest . . . vessel: "Thou shalt krush them with a sceptre of yron; & breake them in pieces like a potters vessel" (Ps. 2.9).

22. For . . . it: "Surely mine enemie did not disfame me: for I colde have borne it: nether did mine adversarie exalt him self against me: for I wolde have hid me from him" (Ps. 55.12).

23. Senacherib: A great Assyrian king who attempted a seige of Jerusalem against Hezekiah. He failed in this, but he managed to remove an enormous tribute, including Temple treasures (2 Kings 18ff.).

24. Esau's . . . TEA: Esau was the son of Isaac and Rebekah and the older brother of Jacob. Stories about the two dwell on Jacob's trickery over Esau. One time Esau was hungry, and he lost his birthright privileges when his brother offered to buy them with a mess of pottage (Gen. 25.29–34).

25. They . . . season: "For he shalbe like a tre planted by the rivers of waters, that wil bring forthe her frute in due season: whose leafe shal not fade: so whatsoever he shal do, shal prosper" (Ps. 1.3).

26. 3.36: "The pride of thine heart hathe deceived thee: thou that dwellest in the cleftes of the rockes, whose habitacion is hie, that saith in his heart, Who shal bring me downe to the grounde? Yea thogh thou exalt thy self as the egle, & make thy nest among the starres, thence wil I bring thee downe, saith the Lord"; "All the men of thy confederacie have driven thee to the borders: the men that were at peace with thee, have deceived thee, and prevailed against thee: thei that eat thy bread, have laid a wounde under thee: there is none understanding in him" (Obad. 3–4, 7).

27. Pride . . . fall: "Pride goeth before destruction, and an high minde before the fall" (Prov. 16.18).

28. it is . . . meddling: "It is a mans honour to cease from strife: but everie foole wil be medling" (Prov. 20.3).

29. seeing . . . flesh: "I wil make mine arrowes dronke with blood, (and my sworde shal eat flesh) for the blood of the slaine, & of the captives, when I begin to take vengeance of the enemy" (Deut. 32.42).

30. Matherius Cottonius: Cotton Mather (1663–1728) countenanced the witchcraft trials and executions of 1692–93. He actively opposed the royal governor, Sir Edmund Andros (1637–1714), here fictionalized as Balaam.

31. Balaam the wizzard: Balaam was a heathen occultist. He was summoned by Balak, King of Moab, to invoke a curse upon Israel, whose tribes were advancing into the Jordan Valley. His story presents the image of a pagan man sensitive to God's commands (Num. 22–24). Balaam represents Andros, who, after having been governor of the province of New York, was appointed in 1686 to be governor of the Dominion of New England. Andros interfered with the colonists' rights and customs; in 1689, the colonists revolted and imprisoned him. He was sent back to England, where the charges against him were never pressed (*WBD*).

32. 3.42–46: "Therefore Saul asked counsel of the Lord, & the Lord answered him not, nether by dreames, nor by Urim, nor yet by Prophetes. Then said Saul unto his servants, Seke me a woman that hathe a familiar spirit, that I may go to her, and aske of her. And his servants said to him, Beholde, there is a woman at En-dor that hathe a familiar spirit. Then Saul changed him selfe, and put on other raiment, and he went, and two men with him, and they came to the woman by night: and he said, I pray thee, conjecture unto me by the familiar spirit, and bring me up whome I shal name unto thee" (1 Sam. 28.6–8).

33. Carey: Later called "sister" Carey (3.55) and "Mother" Carey (3.57). Elizabeth Cary (wife of Nathaniel Cary, one of the selectmen of Charlestown and a General Court representative) was arraigned and tried as a witch in the 1690s. Elizabeth Cary escaped from prison in Cambridge and fled to Rhode Island and then to New York, where she died 30 August 1722 (Winsor 1:314).

In the entry for *Mother Carey's Chickens*, Brewer has stated that "Mother Carey is *mata cara*, dear mother. The French call these birds *oiseaux de Notre Dame* or *aves Sanctae Mariae.*" The name, then, seems to have been derived from sacred implications.

Leacock's Mother Carey is amorous and obliging. This aspect of her character probably relates to another meaning for *mother Carey's chickens* perhaps available in Leacock's time. (Brewer's *Dict.*; McCarter, 171). See the Introduction (re: John Hancock) and note 15, chapter 5.

34. behold . . . die: "And the woman said unto him, Beholde, thou knowest what Saul hathe done, how he hathe destroyed the sorcerers, and the sothesayers out of the land: wherefore then sekest thou to take me in to cause me to dye?" (1 Sam. 28.9).

35. Knowest . . . new: "Therefore if anie man be in Christ, let him be a new creature. Olde things are passed away: beholde, all things are become new" (2 Cor. 5.17).

36. 3.58–59: "Then said the woman, Whome shal I bring up unto thee? And he answered, Bring me up Samuel" (1 Sam. 28.11).

37. OLIVER CROMWELL: Cromwell, Lord Protector of England (1638–58), led the Puritan cause against Catholicism and Anglicanism; Cromwell's power gave the later Puritans an image of themselves as an outpost of the Reformation (Bercovitch, *Am. Jer.*, 5, 68).

38. 3.59–64: "And when the woman sawe Samuel, she cryed with a loude voyce, and the woman spake to Saul, saying, Why hast thou deceived me? for thou art Saul. And the King said unto her, Be not afrayed: for what sawest thou? And the woman said unto Saul, I sawe gods ascending up out of the earth. Then he said unto her, What facion is he of? And she answered, An olde man cometh up lapped in a mantel: and Saul knewe that it was Samuel, and he enclined his face to the ground, & bowed him selfe. And Samuel said to Saul, Why hast thou disquieted me, to bring me up? Then Saul answered, I am in great distress: for the Philistims make warre against me, & God is departed from me, and answereth me nomore, nether by Prophetes nether by dreames: therefore I have called thee, that thou mayest tel me, what I shal do" (1 Sam. 28.12–15).

39. with . . . rhinoceros: Before he was named Lord Protector, Cromwell had been known for his simple if not shoddy dress. When he received the title, however, Cromwell took evident pleasure in dressing regally. Royalist pamphleteers often mocked Cromwell's looks, especially his large nose and his warts (Fraser, 62–64, 230–31, 325, 472, 577).

Chapter 4

1. Moreover . . . Levi: The most active loyalist opposition came from New York, where the Episcopalian clergymen—Samuel Seabury, Miles Cooper, Thomas Chandler, and Charles Inglis, among others—ran an active campaign against the patriots and the First Continental Congress (Becker, 158–59).

2. Coo-r-ites . . . Addresser: Reverend Dr. Miles Cooper was much disliked by the patriots. In May 1774, William Lee informed the colonies of his knowledge of specific bribes that the ministry was offering for loyal support in the colonies. Most of the money was to be spent in New York. Cooper, President of King's College, was promised consecration as the first American bishop (Bridenbaugh, 253, 324–26; Launitz-Schurer, 140–42). See also 4.7. On 13 October 1771, Cooper made a trip to London, carrying various petitions from colonial clergymen who wished to establish an American episcopate. News of this voyage traveled fast, and apprehensions and animosities increased as reports came in that Cooper had joined forces with Reverend James Horrocks in petitioning for American bishops (Bridenbaugh, 324, 327).

A Friendly Address to All Reasonable Americans on the Subject of our Political Confusions: in which the Necessary Consequences of Violently Opposing the King's Troops and of a general Non-Importation are fairly stated was published for the first time in New York between the middle of September and the middle of October 1774. Although this anonymous pamphlet was actually written by Thomas Bradbury Chandler, it was often ascribed to Cooper (Becker, 279–80, 159; see also Bailyn, *Origins*, 313–14).

3. R----g--n . . . Presser: James Rivington, printer of the *New York Gazeteer*, a paper distinguished for its pro-administration policy, was named King's Printer in April 1775, at an annual salary of £100. This function enabled the patriot spy Rivington—who continued to act as if in favor of the ministry—to receive and transmit to Washington and other patriots the latest British measures (Crary; Launitz-Schurer, 142). See 4.7.

4. making . . . pamphlets: A pamphlet war between loyalist and patriot supporters began shortly after the First Continental Congress. In New York, the Episcopal clergy denounced the Congress as having betrayed America (Becker, 158–59).

5. they . . . clothing: "Beware of false prophetes, which come to you in shepe's clothing, but inwardely they are ravening wolves" (Matt. 7.15).

6. purified . . . beard: Aaron, the first head of the Hebrew priesthood, was anointed by Moses.

7. make . . . charter: The Massachusetts Charter of 1629, the original colonial charter from Charles I, gave a constitutional basis for a holy commonwealth beyond the king's reach, by granting legislative power and the power of election to the colony itself. After the Glorious Revolution, Massachusetts had to accept in 1691 a new charter giving legislative power to the colony but calling for governors to be royally appointed. In addition, these governors could negative elected members' admittance to the Council and the General Court. At the time of the First Continental Congress, many Massachusetts radicals wished to resume the rights granted by the original charter (1629), arguing that the King did not have as extensive an authority when dealing with the British Parliament itself (Miller, 21; Jensen, 501).

8. conscience . . . offence: "And herein I endevour my self to have alway a cleare conscience toward God, & towarde men" (Acts 24.16).

9. how . . . greatness: Royalist Edward Hyde, Earl of Clarendon, admitted that Cromwell's greatness at home was a mere shadow to his greatness abroad. Bishop Burnet, too, told of Cromwell's traditional boast that he would make the name of Englishman as great as ever that of Roman had been (*DNB*).

10. hustled . . . about: Using force, Cromwell secured Ireland and Scotland as Commonwealth lands. These victories for the Commonwealth assured the recognition of the republic by foreign states (*DNB*).

11. swayed . . . hands: By making treaties with the United Provinces, and especially with Denmark and Portugal, Cromwell made great gains for English merchants, who were ensured toleration and free trade. Cromwell later joined with France, against Spain. He complemented this alliance with one with Sweden. He felt it necessary to support Sweden to maintain the freedom of the Baltic and protect English trade there (*DNB*). See note 14 below.

12. banished . . . land: Cromwell, though he was strongly anti-Catholic in his administration in Ireland, encouraged liberty of conscience in religious concerns. Apologists for his rule boasted of the freedom of conscience enjoyed under it. Detractors found less toleration than they wished. With all its defects and restrictions, the religious liberty maintained by the Protector was far in advance of average public opinion even among those of his own party (*DNB*).

13. shook . . . woodpecker: Perhaps an allusion to Cromwell's gain over Catholicism ("his Holiness"), in the defeat of England's Charles I ("the great dragon" in symbol), who ruled over England, Ireland, and Scotland (the "tripple crown") and who allowed the free exercise of the Roman Catholic religion and enforced the toleration of Catholics. See notes 10 and 12 above.

14. suffered . . . king: In the decision whether to ally England to France or to Spain, Cromwell considered the close family relationship of the Stuarts to the French king. The Anglo-French commercial treaty of October 1655 shows how Cromwell was able to deter possible French pretensions to the English throne; each side agreed not to help those

rebels (including Charles Stuart) "now declared" in the other's country. This agreement precluded French aid to the Stuarts, and some secret clauses of the treaty provided for Charles II and some other prominent royalists to be expelled from France (Fraser, 540–41).

15. invincible . . . Spaniard: Perhaps a reference to Blake's seizure, under Cromwell's orders, of the Spanish fleet at Santa Cruz. See note 16 below.

16. despised . . . sea: Two great victories of England over the Spanish treasure fleets were much celebrated. The first, in September 1656, was the destruction of a treasure fleet by Captain Richard Stayner. The more resounding victory, however, was that of Blake in April 1657, at the port of Santa Cruz, where he fell upon the Spanish fleet, completely demolished it, and gained a victory that was likened to the defeat of the Spanish Armada (Fraser, 543).

17. sly . . . states: Perhaps an allusion to the Navigation Act of 1651, aimed at destroying the Dutch monopoly of trade, by which the Dutch conceded the supremacy of the English flag (*DNB*).

18. strong . . . flag: Cromwell dispatched Blake to control the Mediterranean in 1654–1655, literally by showing the British flag. Blake made Algiers turn over its English captives, and his fleet made English trade secure on the Mediterranean (*DNB*; Fraser, 537).

19. He that . . . us: "He that is not with me, is against me: & he that gathereth not with me, scattereth"; "For whosoever is not against us, is on our parte" (Matt. 12.30; Mark 9.40).

20. break . . . you: "Let us breake their bands, and cast their cords from us" (Ps. 2.3).

21. witness . . . Moor: Nearly defeated by the royalist army in the battle at Marston Moor, the parliamentary army rallied and made a resounding defeat of the royalists. Cromwell's charge into the midst of Goring's retiring cavalry is said to have ensured parliamentary success (*DNB*).

22. Haman . . . Northite: Haman is the villain of the Esther narrative. He was a persecutor of the Jews, and he received the punishment that he had plotted for them. See note 26, chapter 2.

23. heads . . . served: In 1660 the Convention Parliment ruled that Cromwell's body, among others, be disinterred. In January 1661, on the twelfth anniversary of the king's execution, Cromwell's body was hung on the gallows at Tyburn. His head was later set up on a pole on the top of Westminster Hall (*DNB*).

24. 4.20: "But rise and stand up on thy fete: for I have appeared unto thee for this purpose, to appoint thee a minister and a witnes, bothe of the things which thou hast sene, & of the things in the which I will appeare unto thee" (Acts 26.16).

25. whet . . . spears: "And he shal judge among many people, & rebuke mightie nacions a farre of, & thei shal breake their swordes into mattockes, and their speares into sieths: nacion shal not lift up a sworde against nacion, nether shal they learne to fight any more" (Mic. 4.3).

26. Fairfax: Ferdinando Fairfax (1584–1648) commanded the Parliamentary forces in Yorkshire and fought in the battle of Marston Moor (*DNB*).

27. Lambert: John Lambert (1619–83) led the cavalry at Marston Moor and fought successfully in Scotland. He led the council of officers that installed Cromwell as Lord Protector (*DNB*).

28. A PROCLAMATION: On 28 September 1774, Gage presented a proclamation proroguing the General Court. (The proclamation is printed among the documents in Appendix C.) The patriots were enraged by Gage's change of mind concerning the General Court meeting. When by mid-September it seemed clear that Gage would not allow the Court to meet, many towns prepared for a Provincial Congress to be held at Concord, and they elected two sets of representatives. Evidently, ninety representatives

gathered in Salem for the General Court meeting. They waited three days for the governor to appear. When Gage did not appear for the meeting, they voted a series of resolves condemning the proclamation of 28 September as unconstitutional, calling his remarks "injurious and unkind." They formally resolved for a Provincial Congress and adjourned to Concord (Patterson, 109–10).

29. *without . . . thereunto:* Even before the King's execution, a new Great Seal had been put into use by the Commons at a cost of £200. The new seal (established by a committee of the Commons) made clear the change in the seat of power: on one side was shown the House of Commons and its Speaker (no House of Lords); and on the other, the words, "In the First Year of Freedom by God's blessing restored 1648" (Fraser, 299, 456–57).

30. *council: Fairfax:* see note 26 above. *Ireton:* Henry Ireton (1611–51), Cromwell's son-in-law, took part in the cavalry at Naseby and in the Irish campaign. He signed the death warrant for the execution of Charles I. *Willoughby:* Francis Willoughby, fifth Baron Willoughby of Parham (1613?–66), fought with Manchester's troops and helped capture Bolingbroke Castle. He later turned to the King's side. *Zankey:* I have been unable to identify Zankey. Perhaps a pun on "Yankee"? *Skippon:* Philip Skippon (d. 1660) was popular among the parliamentary troops for his encouragement. He wrote three books of devotions for his soldiers. One of the King's judges, he did not use his power. *Hammond:* Robert Hammond (1621–54) took part in the battle at Naseby, was captured during the seige of Basing House, and escaped. He broke with the military in 1647, when the army tried to use force against Parliament. Cromwell sent him to Ireland, where he died. *Rainsborough:* The Rainsborough brothers, Thomas and William, fought on the side of parliament. Both extremist in their views, they opposed negotiations with the King and supported strong military leadership. *Pride:* Thomas Pride (d. 1658) commanded a regiment at Naseby. A regicide, he opposed Cromwell's appointment as King. *Lambert:* see note 27 above. *Coote:* Sir Charles Coote, Earl of Mountrath (d. 1661), a military commander in Ireland, was the ablest friend of the Commonwealth in Ireland. *Venables:* Robert Venables (1612–87) worked with Coote in the Irish campaign. *Broghill:* Roger Boyle, Baron Broghill and first Earl of Orrery (1621–79), held a general's command in Ireland under Cromwell. He was a dramatist as well. *Hewson:* John Hewson (d. 1662), a regicide, took part in the Irish campaign. *Abbot:* Probably a reference to Robert Abbot (1588?–1663?), divine, educated at Cambridge and Oxford. He was a Puritan, although he waged a prolonged warfare with the Brownists. *Reynolds:* John Reynolds (1625–57) took part in the Irish campaign. A zealous supporter of Cromwell, he was knighted by the Protector, and he voted to offer him the crown. *Ewer:* Isaac Ewer (d. 1650), a regicide, fought with the parliamentary army and was given custody of the King at Hurst Castle. *Lilburne:* Two Lilburnes, brothers, fought in the parliamentary army. John (1614–57) was imprisoned in 1637 for procuring and publishing Puritan pamphlets. He attacked Cromwell's Commonwealth as too aristocratic. His brother Robert (1613–65) took part in the Scottish campaigns. He signed the King's death warrant but opposed the idea of making Cromwell king. *Fleetwood:* Charles Fleetwood (d. 1692) took part in the battle at Naseby and became a commander in Ireland. He married Cromwell's daughter Bridget, widow of Henry Ireton. *Desborough:* John Desborough (1608–80) nearly captured Charles II after the battle of Worcester. He is caricatured in Butler's *Hudibras*. *Harrison:* Thomas Harrison (1606–60) fought on the parliamentary side and advocated the trial of Charles I. He escorted the King from Hurst Castle to London and signed his death warrant. He held chief command in England during Cromwell's absence. *Blake:* Robert Blake (1599–1657) is best known for his successes at sea. See notes 15, 16, and 18 above. *Gibbons:* Perhaps a reference to Christopher Gibbons (1615–76), a composer whom Cromwell may have patronized during the Protectorate, due to his delight in masques and musical entertainments. *Marsh:* I have been unable to identify Marsh. *Jones:* Michael Jones (d. 1649) took part in the Irish campaigns (*DNB*; Fraser, 465–66).

31. John Bradshaw: Bradshaw (1602–59), English judge and regicide, presided at the trial of Charles I and pronounced the death sentence. Censured by the crowds of royalist pamphleteers for his overbearing behavior toward the King, Bradshaw was praised by Milton and considered by Americans one of the principal victims of Stuart tyranny.

Perhaps Leacock knew of Franklin's mock epitaph on Bradshaw. Although the earliest known printing of the "Epitaph" is in Benjamin Towne's *Pennsylvania Evening Post* of 14 December 1775, it might have circulated in manuscript prior to that date. It was probably printed as a broadside in December 1775 or later. Jefferson admired the work (*DNB*; Jefferson, *Papers* 1:677–79).

32. Colonel . . . Congress: Hancock, wealthy Boston merchant and radical, took the leading part as the "submitter" of the Whately letters. When the General Court changed to the Provincial Congress, Hancock was chosen President. See the Introduction.

33. ONE . . . TENOR: Colonial paper money fluctuated in value, depending on its standard. Before 1750, the Massachusetts colony used "lawful money" geared to the Spanish dollar. At other times, it used old, middle, and new tenor paper money that had started as "lawful money" and depreciated. After 1750, the colony went back to a lawful money expressed in both Spanish and English silver, and this money did not depreciate (Brown, 83).

Chapter 5

1. every . . . neighbour: "Everie man helped his neighbour and said to his brother, Be strong" (Isa. 41.6).

2. 5.4–16: A well-publicized tea consignment incident occurred in Annapolis, Maryland. On Friday, 14 October 1774, the *Peggy Stewart*, owned by Anthony Stewart and his father-in-law James Dick, arrived at Annapolis with over 2,000 pounds of tea. Stewart—for himself, Dick, and Joseph Williams, the tea consignees—paid the tea duty at the customs house. The same afternoon, four members of the Anne Arundel County Committee of Observation called a mass meeting and ordered that the tea not be landed, although the rest of the cargo could be. On Wednesday, 19 October, Stewart, Dick, and Williams appeared at the Committee's second meeting and offered to burn the tea. The Committee agreed that burning—and a public apology—would be adequate punishment. When extremists insisted the ship also be burned, Stewart decided to burn the ship also, for the sake of his family's safety. He set the blaze himself. Stewart, Dick, and Williams signed an apology declaring that they had committed an insult to the liberties of America (Jensen, 520).

3. Grand Congress: The popular name for the First Continental Congress. See the newspaper accounts, note 8 below.

4. Thomas the Cushingite: Thomas Cushing's first patriot act was in organizing the colonies against the Stamp Act. Franklin transmitted to him the Whately letters, which further implicated Cushing in radical activity. In July 1774 he became part of the Committee of Safety in Boston. A handbill issued in 1774 included Cushing among those charged with treason against the British government. He was elected to the Provincial Congress and to the First Continental Congress. He strongly urged measures against importation, consumption, and exportation (*DAB*).

5. Adamites: Samuel and John Adams were leading patriots.

6. Robert the Painite: Robert Treat Paine attended the Provincial Congress and served as a member of the First Continental Congress.

7. like . . . Solomon: Cassia is the aromatic bark of a tree similar to cinnamon, though less delicate in flavor. The Queen of Sheba's visits to Solomon are narrated in 1 Kings 10.1, 4, 10, 13; 2 Chron. 9.1, 3, 9, 12.

8. since . . . Louisburgh: After having noted congressional news as it arrived, the *Boston Gazette* (in its 31 October and 7 November issues) also reported on the delegates' pending arrival back home. Its 14 November notice of the delegates' return home announced:

> Last Wednesday evening arrived in town, the Hon. Thomas Cushing, Esq: Mr. Samuel Adams, and John Adams, Esq: Delegates from this province, to the late GRAND AMERICAN CONGRESS. The people testified their joy at their safe arrival, by ringing of bells, &c.

Similar reports were run in the *Massachusetts Spy* (10 November) and the *Boston Post-Boy* (14 November).

9. Simon: The biblical reference is probably to Simon Magnus, who was guilty of the sins of trafficking in sacred things and buying and selling religious offices (Acts 8.18).

10. For . . . rest: Evidently, this is Leacock's verse.

11. Monsieur . . . Bearda: The patriots disliked England's relations with France. They especially disliked the Quebec Act, which gave governing power to the French Catholics who had settled in Canada.

12. Philistians . . . thee: "(And she had men lying in wayte with her in the chamber) Then she said unto him, The Philistims be upon thee, Samson. And he brake the cordes, as a thread of towe is broken, when it feleth fire: so his strength was not knowen" (Judg. 16.9).

John Andrews's letters reveal much about the British treatment of deserters. On 15 August 1774, he wrote, "Every humane person was pleas'd to be inform'd that the military were not suffer'd to punish a deserter with a death; but when we find that a thousand lashes is a substitute, we are equally shock'd to think that mankind can so far divest themselves of humanity as to be instrumental in inflicting such an horrid punishment on their fellow mortals. . . . They are kept under much stricter discipline than if in an enemy's country; being put under guard if seen conversing with an inhabitant, and not suffer'd to leave the camp without a written pass, which makes the soldiers very dissatisfied with their situation, and rather stimulates their going off than otherways" (28–29). By 30 November, Andrews wrote: "The desertions have been so great of late that the troops had orders last evening to call the roll every half hour till further orders" (45). On 24 December, desertions had reached such a pitch that Gage was "determin'd to make an example of" a deserter by shooting him (79). A letter of 27 January 1775 brought this comment from Andrews: "Its shocking to conceive to what degree the soldiers are punish'd. Its imagin'd half their deaths arise from it, as it often happens that their ribs are laid quite bare, whereby their kidneys are so affected that they become incurable" (84).

13. Old Boy: The Devil. "And the great dragon, that olde serpent, called the devil and Satan, was cast out, which deceiveth all the worlde: he was even cast into the earth, & his Angels were cast out with him"; "And he toke the dragon that olde serpent, which is the devil and Satan, and he bounde him a thousand yeres" (Rev. 12.9; 20.2).

14. Lapland witches: The Lapps' reputation as sorcerers was partly derived from the *History of the Northern Peoples* (1555), in which Olaus Magnus, Archbishop of Uppsala, described the magical practices of these people. Milton referred to the Lapland witches when describing Hell in *Paradise Lost*. 2.62–66 (*Man, Myth, Magic*).

15. mother Carey's chickens: See note 33, chapter 3, for the sacred derivation of "Mother Carey." The most common meaning for *Mother Carey's chickens*, used at least as early as 1767, is a simple reference to one of the various petrels, especially the stormy petrel, so named by sailors (*Cent. Dict.*; *DAE*; *OED*). The term can also refer to falling snow (Brewer's *Dict.*; *OED*). Still another use of the term might be in reference to prostitutes or a house of prostitution, a meaning found by 1807 (*DAE*). See the Introduction.

16. shadow . . . substance: Perhaps slur against a particular eighteenth-century philosophy concerning the nature of reality, but more likely (here and in the verses following) one against medieval Catholic scholasticism, in which reason was subservient to faith, a belief taught in the Catholic Church.

During the eighteenth century, scholasticism came under attack by philosophers who said that scholasticism consisted of the vain speculations of the dark ages, when the human mind was the slave of Aristotle and the papacy. The scholastic method followed a general pattern: first, the text under consideration was broken into a number of propositions; second, questions about the text were raised and a variety of possible answers set forth; third, arguments, pro and con, were adduced in a syllogistic chain, leading to a conclusion. By developing arguments in this manner, scholastic philosophers believed they could demonstrate certain natural truths. They also believed, however, in ethical truths, "of grace," not of nature, which were revealed, not discoverable. This doctrine of twofold truth allowed that some things were true according to reason, although the opposite could be true according to faith.

The eighteenth-century critics of this philosophy saw as ridiculous the schoolmen's ability to develop various propositions that could be untrue either according to reason or according to faith (*Dict. of Philos. and Psych.*).

17. I . . . judged: "Judge not, that ye be not judged" (Matt. 7.1).

18. speaking . . . ass: Balaam is rebuked by his ass (Num. 22.28; 2 Peter 2.16). See note 31, chapter 3.

19. witch . . . Samuel: See 3.44–48.

20. dispute . . . appearance: This is perhaps a slur against the scholastic confusion about the nature of reality; admitting that universals are the real in the mind of God, and the archetypes of all created things, the scholastic philosophers had difficulty relating these concepts to the sensible world (*Dict. of Philos. and Psych.*).

21. two . . . paper: Perhaps an allusion to the Ossian controversy. In 1760, Macpherson published *Fragments* and *Poems of Ossian*. These were widely acclaimed. Hume, for instance, liked the poems, although he later objected that they could not have been preserved intact. And although Samuel Johnson denounced them as forgeries from the outset, in his *Journey to the Western Islands of Scotland* (published January 1775), he spent some time discussing their authorship (see Rubel).

22. 5.47–48: Early in November 1774, merchant John Norton brought his ship *Virginia*, loaded with two half-chests of tea consigned to Williamsburg merchants, into the York River, and he docked it at Yorktown. Enraged, the local patriots pressed for action against Norton. The York committee (with Norton's friend Thomas Nelson in the chair), after having discarded a plan to burn the *Virginia*, decided to destroy the tea and send the vessel off without allowing it to take on its expected cargo of tobacco. On 7 November, the committee boarded the ship, and Nelson threw the tea in the York River (Evans).

Chapter 6

1. 6. 1–3: "And when he shal sit upon the throne of his kingdome, then shal he write him this Lawe repeted in a boke, by the Priests of the Levites. And it shalbe with him, and he shal read therein all the dayes of his life, that he may learne to feare the Lord his God, & to kepe all the wordes of this Lawe, and these ordinances, for to do them: That his heart be not lifted up above his brethren, and that he turne not from the commandment, to the right hand or to the left, but that he may prolong his dayes in his kingdome, he, and his sonnes in the middes of Israel" (Deut. 17.18–20).

2. strive . . . servants: An inversion of the text (Isa. 45.9; Jer. 50.24; Matt. 12.19; 2 Tim. 2.24).

3. Solomon thy grandfather: Solomon, the third king of Israel, was known for his wisdom and for the splendor of his court. See notes 14 and 15, chapter 2.

4. Pitites: William Pitt, Earl of Chatham (1708–78), became known as the Great Commoner for his championing of colonial rights at the time of the Stamp Act crisis. Pitt spoke in favor of a bill for the relief of dissenters in May 1772, and he made a violent attack against the bishops. He sought a pacific solution to colonial problems and consulted with Franklin concerning viable options. In May through June 1774, Pitt asserted that the British government had no right to tax the colonists, and he denounced the Quebec Act. In January 1775, Pitt proposed an address to the King to request his recall of the troops in Boston and to show his justification for the colonial resistance (*DNB*). Leacock celebrated Pitt as a folk hero in *A New Song, On the Repeal of the Stamp-Act* (1766). See Mulford.

5. thou . . . men: "And the King answered the people sharpely, and left the olde mens counsel that thei gave him" (1 Kings 12.13).

6. Thy . . . feet: "Then the young men that were broght up with him, spake unto him, saying, Thus shalt thou say unto this people, that have spoken unto thee, and said, Thy father hathe made our yoke heavie, but make thou it lighter unto us: even thus shalt thou say unto them, My least parte shalbe bigger then my fathers loynes. Now where as my father did burden you with a grievous yoke, I wil yet make your yoke heavier: my father hathe chastised you with rods, but I wil correct you with scourges" (1 Kings 12.10–11). See a similar passage, 2.13; see also 1 Kings 12.4, 14.

7. encouraged . . . calves: Idolatrous groves and golden calves were forbidden. See for example Deut. 16.21; Judg. 6.25.

8. in . . . Quebeckites: Catholics were ensured toleration by the Quebec Act.

9. immortal Wolfe: James Wolfe (1727–59), a British army officer, served in Flanders and Germany against the Young Pretender (1742–47), and, under Amherst, he played a brilliant part in the seige of Louisburg (1758). He commanded with the rank of major-general the expedition against Quebec (1759). He scaled the heights to the Plains of Abraham, routed the French under Montcalm, and thus served a major role in the completion of the British conquest of North America. He fell mortally wounded on the field in that battle. That Wolfe died in battle against the French made him seem to the colonists like a martyr when England later restored power to the French in the Quebec Act (*DNB*).

10. Louis . . . France: Perhaps an allusion to Louis XIV, who gradually deprived the Huguenots of their rights. When the Edict of Nantes was revoked (1685), thousands fled France (*WBD*).

11. Carolus . . . Hispania: Probably a reference to Charles V, a Holy Roman Emperor, who was tolerant of protestants in Germany but who persecuted them in Spain (*WBD*).

12. Pope . . . Hildebrand: Gregory Hildebrand, Pope Gregory VII, aimed as Pope to establish the supremacy of the papacy within the church and of the church over the state (*WBD*).

13. Ophir: An unidentified region, famous in Old Testament stories for its fine gold. See Gen. 10.29; 1 Kings 10.11.

14. do we . . . Peru: When the Caribbean area could no longer absorb all the goods exported by the colonies, the colonists began to export to Spain, Portugal, and the Wine Islands off the African coast. It was an extremely profitable trade, because while the colonists exported wheat, corn, flour, fish, lumber, rum, and rice, they usually brought back only wine and salt. The heavy balances in their favor were paid in cash and bills of exchange. Limited by law in their payments for imports from England by using direct exports, the American merchants could use cash gained from these other areas of trade to pay off their debt to England (Jensen, 17–18).

15. Moreover . . . ambassador: The Massachusetts Bay petitions were discounted in Privy Council; Franklin was dishonored.

16. almost . . . old: Saint Stephen was the first Christian martyr. False witnesses accused him of unholiness, and a mob seized him and stoned him to death. His death marks the end of the early phase of Christianity (*Bible Dict.*).

17. like . . . Vesuvius: Etna is an active volcano in Catania province on the eastern coast of Sicily. Sixteen eruptions of Etna were recorded during the eighteenth century. Vesuvius is an active volcano rising above the Bay of Naples. Six eruptions were recorded for the eighteenth century; two of them took place during the 1760s. (*Encyclopaedia Britannica, A New Survey of Useful Knowledge*, edited by Walter Yust et al., 24 vols. [Chicago: Encyclopaedia Britannica, 1960]).

18. (were . . . land): Two of the Coercive Acts affected colonial right to self-rule. The Massachusetts Government Act (enacted April 1774) removed all governing responsibilities from colonial hands and gave the power of election and appointment to royal appointees. The Administration of Justice Act (enacted May 1774) provided that royally appointed governors, magistrates, and other officials could only be tried in England if they were convinced that a fair trial could not be had in Massachusetts (Jensen, 456–58). The colonists argued that their right of self-government had been granted with the original 1629 charter, which was revoked and changed at the time of the Glorious Revolution. See note 7, chapter 4.

19. scalded . . . exotic: When the Tea Act was issued in 1773, some newspapers printed attacks on the use of tea itself. One writer declared that tea was an evil, dangerous, and "unconstitutional" drink. Another warned that a flea-like insect could be found in shipped tea. And Dr. Thomas Young of Boston assured his readers that the newspaper writers who called tea a "pernicious drug" were wrong; "the sober truth," he asserted, "is that tea is really a slow poison" (quoted in Jensen, 440).

20. Belzebub . . . holiness: In the New Testament, the Pharisees call Beelzebub the "prince of the devils" (Matt. 12.24). *Bellwether* is the term used contemptuously in relation to a clamorous person ready to speak up (*OED*).

21. bishops: The colonists did not wish to see the establishment of the Anglican church—though the first settlers were themselves members of the church—in the colonies. When in 1763 it seemed as if an Anglican Episcopate might have arisen in the colonies, the well-organized Committees of Correspondence relayed news and agitated for resistance until the defeat of the Anglican-backed Stamp Act. Perhaps the greatest fear of an Anglican Episcopate occurred 1766 through 1770 in New York, where mounting Anglican militancy and political activity brought about the defeat of the Presbyterians in their 1768 request for incorporation (Bridenbaugh, 230–87). Having come to associate liberty with protestantism (as opposed to what they saw as the combination of arbitrary power and popery), New England ministers, patriots, and pamphleteers saw the Coercive Acts, the Quebec Act, and the proposed Anglican bishopric only as different branches of the same scheme of tyranny established in Rome (Hatch, 52, 55–96, esp. 73–75).

22. society . . . propaganda: The missionary group of the Church of England was the Society for the Propagation of the Gospel in Foreign Parts.

23. devils . . . horns: "And I sawe a beast rise out of the sea, having seven heads, and ten hornes, and upon his hornes were ten crownes, and upon his heads the name of blasphemie" (Rev. 13.1). See also Dan. 7.2, 7; Rev. 12.3 and 17.3, 9, 12.

24. out . . . trees: "We hanged our harpes upon the willowes in the middes thereof" (Ps. 137.2).

25. have . . . primers: The *New England Primer* usually included a woodcut (which varied), depicting the martyrdom of John Rogers, along with an explanation like the following one, taken from the earliest known edition of the *Primer*:

106   Notes to the Text

> Mr. John Rogers, Minister of the Gospel in London, was the first Martyr in Q Mary's Reign, and was burnt at Smithfield, February the fourteenth, 1554[.] His Wife, with nine small Children, and one at her Breast, following him to the Stake, with which sorrowful sight he was not in the least daunted, but with wonderful Patience died couragiously for the Gospel of Jesus Christ.

The woodcut and description often were accompanied by an "exhortation" from Rogers to his children (Ford).

26. John Rodgers: Rogers was sentenced to death as a heretic for having denied the Christian character of the Church of Rome and the real presence in the Sacrament.

27. did . . . King: The delegates to the First Continental Congress developed resolutions and plans of action; they then adopted addresses to the King, to the people of Britain, and to Thomas Gage (Labaree, 199). See note 12, chapter 2.

28. NORTH wind: The colonists blamed North for the Coercive Acts. See note 26, chapter 2.

29. Wo . . . child: "Wo to thee, o land, when thy King is a childe, and thy princes eat in the morning" (Eccles. 10.16).

30. broken . . . clay: "Thou shalt krush them with a sceptre of yron, & breake them in pieces like a potters vessel" (Ps. 2.9).

31. Wo . . . ropes: "Wo unto them, that drawe iniquitie with cordes of vanitie, and sinne as with cart ropes" (Isa. 5.18).

32. sweep . . . sea: Pharoah, oppressor of Israel, perished in the Red Sea (Exod. 14).

33. Babel: The Hebrew name for Babylon.

34. Babylon is fallen: See Isa. 13.14; 21.2, 47, 48; Jer. 25.12, 50, 51.

35. Be . . . earth: "Be wise now therefore, ye Kings: be learned ye Judges of the earth" (Ps. 2.10).

36. kiss . . . peace: "Kisse the Sonne, lest he be angrie, and ye perish in the waie, when his wrath shal suddenly burn. Blessed are all that trust in him" (Ps. 2.12).

37. diligently . . . earth: "If thou shalt obey diligently the voyce of the Lord thy god, and observe and do all his commandements, which I commande thee this day, then the Lord thy God wil set thee on high above all the nacions of the earth" (Deut. 28.1).

38. Blessed . . . field: "Blessed shalt thou be in the citie, & blessed also in the field" (Deut. 28.3).

39. Blessed . . . dough: "Blessed shalbe thy basket and thy dough" (Deut. 28.5).

40. Blessed . . . out: "Blessed shalt thou be, when thou comest in, and blessed also when thou goest out" (Deut. 28.6).

41. Blessed . . . butter: "Blessed shalbe the frute of thy body, & the frute of thy ground, and the frute of thy cattel, the increase of thy kine, & the flockes of thy shepe" (Deut. 28.4). See also Deut. 28.11.

42. Blessed . . . day: Benjamin Franklin had published in Philadelphia (1744) a pamphlet, An Account of the New Invented Pennsylvania Fire-Places, in which he not only described the stove but also detailed the chimney and its ability to draw out smoke effectively. Franklin's continued interest in chimneys and their smoke is demonstrated in a manuscript he completed much later, sent to Jan Ingenhousz 28 August 1785 and read to the American Philosophical Society on October of that year: "On the Causes and Cure of Smoky Chimneys." Another of Franklin's August 1785 manuscripts on the topic, "Description of a New Stove for burning of Pitcoal, and consuming all its Smoke," was read to the Society on 28 January 1786 (Franklin, Papers 2:419–46; Franklin, Writings 9:413–43, 443–63).

43. Then . . . ways: "And the Lord shal cause thee to fall before thine enemies: thou shalt come out one way against them, and shalt flee seven wayes before them, and shalt be scattered through all the kingdomes of the earth" (Deut. 28.25). See also Num. 10.35.

44. false . . . elect: "For false Christs shal rise, and false Prophetes, and shal shewe signes and wonders, to deceive if it were possible, the very elect" (Mark 13.22).

45. and . . . them: "But if thou wilt not obey the voyce of the Lord thy God, to kepe and to do all his commandements & his ordinances, which I commande thee this day, then all these curses shal come upon thee, and overtake thee" (Deut. 28.15).

46. Cursed . . . it: "Cursed shalt thou be in the towne, and cursed also in the field" (Deut. 28.16).

47. Cursed . . . it: "Cursed shal thy basket be, & thy dough" (Deut. 28.17).

48. Cursed . . . it: "Cursed shalt thou be when thou comest in, and cursed also when thou goest out" (Deut. 28.19).

49. Cursed . . . scarcity: "Cursed shalbe the frute of thy body, and the frute of thy land, the increase of thy kine, & the flockes of thy shepe" (Deut. 28.18).

50. Zantippe: Xantippe or Xanthippe, the wife of Socrates, is said to have had such a bad temper that her scoldings have rendered her name proverbial for a conjugal scold (Brewer's *Dict.*).

Appendix A
The Satire and the Play

Internal evidence from *The Fall of British Tyranny* (1776) and *The First Book of the American Chronicles of the Times* (1774–75) indicates their common authorship. A summary of the play might make the discussion that follows more clear.

The first two acts of *The Fall of British Tyranny* consist primarily of speeches, act 1 developing speeches of America's enemies in England, and act 2, those of her supporters there. These sets of speeches set up the two opposing sides, revealing the major propaganda statement of the play—that John Stuart, third Earl of Bute (Lord Paramount in the play) wished to incite revolution so that, with England weakened, he could secure power (with his keys to the treasury) for himself and his Stuart relatives. Act 3, less declamatory than the previous two acts, shows the effects of the new Coercive Acts in America, the tension between Whig and Tory there, and reports of battles. After the highly emotional conclusion of act 3 (where "Clarissa" mourns the death of her husband, General Warren), act 4 reveals Dunmore (Lord Kidnapper) as a perfidious, vicious, self-serving fool. The act concludes with a display of British backbiting after the battle of Bunker's Hill. Act 5 shifts the action to Canada, where Ethan Allen suffers at the hands of General Prescott, and then to Cambridge, where Washington discusses with Generals Lee and Putnam the British atrocities and laments with them the death of Montgomery. The orations of Washington, Lee, and Putnam conclude the play.

In addition to a direct allusion within the play to the *American Chronicles*, other elements contribute to the likelihood that Leacock wrote both play and satire. Both texts use similar fictional devices; both use or mention some of the same biblical persons; and both echo some of the same biblical passages.

Similar fictional devices occur in the play and in the satire. The play characterizes Gage as cowardly and weak (3.4, 5); the satire uses similar characterization (5.28–30, 32). Gage faints in both. Gage's chaplain is a hypocritical sot and glutton in both play (4.6) and satire (5.25, 34ff.). Both play and satire mock scholastic reasoning (play, 3.3; satire, 5.46ff.). And the satire and play contain some remarkably similar phrasings. The section of the satire in which Gage converses with Simon (chaplain) is reflected in the play. After Gage tells Simon of the nightmare about Cromwell, Simon exclaims, "Shadows, phantoms, chimeras, bugbears, the effluvia, of a wild imagination, arise, and drink deep of the stream, and forget all your care" (5.43). Simon then makes a long "proof" that Gage's dream was not imaginary, that Cromwell's appearance was a reality. Strikingly similar words are used in the play when Warren's wife, Clarissa, soliloquizes about her nightmare: "Dreams—fancies—evil bodings—shadows, phantoms, and ghastly visions continually hovering around my pillow, goading and harrowing my soul with the most terrific appearances, not imaginary, but real" (3.6). Clarissa not only repeats some of the same words but mentions the same concepts Simon mentions in the satire. Fictional devices like these suggest common authorship.

The biblical elements common to both works indicate their common author. All but two of the biblical references or echoes in the play are drawn from the same passages as those in the satire. Samson is mentioned in the play (1.4; 2.2; 3.4) and in the satire (1.52). The name is spelled *Sampson* in both. Solomon and his wisdom are mentioned in the play (Preface; 1.2; 4.6). In the satire, the action centers around Jedediah. Jedediah was the name given Solomon by the prophet Nathan. In the satire, then, Solomon and his wisdom are evoked in Jedediah's appearances. Both texts rely upon characterizations of some of the same biblical persons.

More important are the places in both play and satire that contain allusions to the same biblical passages. Bute's (Lord Paramount's) boasts about his power (1.3) resemble Rehoboam's (George III's) posturings in the satire (1.13), and both are modeled on Rehoboam's threats in 1 Kings 12. Indeed this same passage is echoed elsewhere in both play (1.5) and satire (2.13; 6. paragraphs 7–9). Moreover, both texts show allusions to Ecclesiastes 4.12, "a threefold cord is not easily broken" (play, 4.6; satire, 2.35), and to the purified oil running down Aaron's beard, as in Psalm 133.2 (play, 3.6; satire, 4.8). Both also contain allusions to the three biblical passages (Matt. 8.32; Mark 5.13; Luke 8.33) in which Jesus drove the devils out of men and made them enter into a herd of swine (play, 2.2, 3.6; satire, 2.13). And both refer to Balaam and his speaking ass of Numbers 22.21–31 (play, 3.6; satire, 3.41, 5.46ff.). Finally, both play (2.2) and satire (3.33) use Genesis 25.29–34, in which Esau sells his birthright for a mess of pottage. These similar textual uses seem only the most striking of the many kinds of internal evidence indicating the common authorship of *The Fall of British Tyranny* and *The First Book of the American Chronicles of the Times*.

Appendix B
List of Characters

This alphabetically arranged list of characters in *The First Book of the American Chronicles of the Times* is keyed to the mention or the appearance of each character in the satire.

Abbot, 4.28
Adamites, 5.17
Aminadab, 1.35, 42, 47; 2.39, 57; 3.42, 46ff.; 4.19, 26
Anthony, 5.5
Balaam (the wizzard), 3.41; 5.42ff.
Bernard, 2.28; Bernardites, 1.10; 4.7, 10
Blake, 4.28
Broghill, 4.28
Bute, 2.28; Johnny the Butetite, 4.18; 6.7, 9
Caleb, 1.42, 51; 2.57
Carey ("Mother," "sister"), 3.54ff.; 4.5, 24
Carolus (king of Hispania), 6.11
Coo-r-ites, 4.2, 7, 11; 5.23; 6.71
Coote, 4.28
Cromwell, 3.59ff.; 4.5ff.; Oliver, 2.10; 3.38; 4.16; 5.1, 42ff.; Oliverians, 1.42, 59ff.; Lord Protector, 4.12, 28; 5.2
Desborough, 4.28
Diego Surly Phiz (Don), 4.12
Ebenezer, see Israel and Jonathan
Ehud (son of Gera), 2.57
Eleazer, 1.51; see Phineas
Eliphalet, see Jedediah the priest
Ewer, 4.28
Ezekiel, 1.27, 49; 2.57
Fairfax, 4.22, 28
Falsey Benabio (Don), 4.12
Fleetwood, 4.28
Gageites, see Thomas the Gageite

Gera, see Ehud
Gibbons, 4.28
Gregory Hildebrand (Pope), 6.11
Haman, see North
Hammond, 4.28
Harrison, 4.28
Hewson, 4.28
Hezekiah, 1.51
Hutchinson, 2.28; Hutchinsonians, 1.10; 4.7, 10; see Judas the parasite
Ireton, 4.28
Israel (son of Ebenezer), 1.50
J. Hancock (Colonel), 4.28; see Obadiah
James, 5.5
Jedediah the priest (son of Eliphalet), 1.19ff., 27, 35, 42, 47; 2.40ff., 57; 3.42ff.; 4.1ff., 19, 27ff.; 5.1ff.; 6.48, 55
Jedediah the scribe, 1.18
Jeremiah, 1.35; 2.27, 57
Johnny the Butetite, see Bute
Jonathan (son of Ebenezer), 1.27, 50; 2.57
Jones, 4.28
Joseph, 5.5
Joshua, 1.53
Judas the parasite, 2.1; see Hutchinson
Lambert, 4.22, 28
Lilburn, 4.28
Lord the King, see Rehoboam
Louis (king of France), 6.11
Mansfield, 2.28
Marsh, 4.28
Matherius Cottonius, 3.41, 54
Monsieur de la Cutta de Bearda, 5.26ff.
Mordecai (the Benjamite), 1.7ff.; 2.31ff.; 6.41
Nathan, 1.51; 2.57
North, 1.58; Haman the Northite, 4.18, 5.13; 6.7, 9
Obadiah, 1.27, 35, 42, 48; 2.57; 3.14ff., 42, 45ff.;4.4, 19, 25; see J. Hancock
Occunneocogeecococacheecacheecadungo, 2.16ff., 35; 4.22
Oliverians, see Cromwell
Othniel, 2.57
Pelatiah, 1.52; 2.57; 3.23
Phineas (son of Eleazer), 2.57; 3.27ff.; 4.21; 6.55
Pitites, 6.6, 7
Pride, 4.28
R----g--n, 4.2, 7; 5.23; R-g-n-ites, 4.11, 6.71

Rainsborough, 4.28
Rehoboam, 2.11ff.; Lord the King, 1.2; address to him, 6
Reuben, 1.51; 2.57
Reynolds, 4.28
Robert the Painite, 5.17
Simon, 5.24ff.
Skippon, 4.28
Thomas the Cushingite, 5.17
Thomas the Gageite, 1.15, 23ff., 55ff.; 3.10, 13, 21ff., 35, 39; Thomas surnamed the Gageite, 2.1ff.; 4.28; 5.24; Thomas the Usurper, 4.14, 28; Gageites, 2.45
Venables, 4.28
Wedderburnite, 1.11
Willoughby, 4.28
Wolf, 6.10
Zankey, 4.28
Zechariah, 1.53; 2.57
Zedekiah, 1.52

Appendix C
Selected Documents

1. Thomas Gage's "Proclamation for the Encouragement of Piety and Virtue."

Issued in July 1774, the proclamation was published in *The Massachusetts Spy*, 28 July 1774:

MASSACHUSETTS-BAY.

By the GOVERNOR.
A PROCLAMATION

For the Encouragement of Piety and Virtue, and for preventing and punishing of Vice, Profanity and Immorality.

In humble imitation of the laudable example of our most gracious Sovereign GEORGE the third, who in the last year of his reign was pleased to issue his royal proclamation for the encouragement of piety and virtue, and for preventing of vice and immorality, in which he declares his royal purpose to punish all persons guilty thereof; and upon all occasions to bestow marks of his royal favour on persons distinguished for their piety and virtue:

I therefore, by and with the advice of his Majesty's council, publish this proclamation, exhorting all his Majesty's subjects to avoid all Hypocrisy, Sedition, Licentiousness, and all other immoralities, and to have a grateful sense of all God's Mercies, making the divine law the rule of their conduct.

I therefore command all Judges, Justices, Sheriffs, and other officers, to use their utmost endeavours to enforce the laws for promoting religion & virtue, and restraining all vice and sedition; and I earnestly recommend to all ministers of the Gospel that they be vigilant and active inculcating a due submission to the laws of God and man; and I exhort all the people of this province, by every means in their power, to contribute what they can towards a general reformation of manners, restitution of peace and good order, and a proper subjection to the laws, as they expect the blessing of Heaven.

And I do farther declare, that in the disposal of the offices of honor and trust, within this province, the supporters of true religion and good government shall be considered as the fittest objects of such appointments.

And I hereby require the Justices of Assise, and Justices of the peace in this province, to give strict charge to the grand jurors for the prosecution of offenders against the laws: And that, in their several courts they cause this proclamation to be publicly read immediately before the charge is given.

Given at the Council chamber in Salem, the 21st day of July, 1774, in the fourteenth Year of the reign of our Sovereign Lord GEORGE *the third, by the Grace of* GOD, *of Great Britain, France and Ireland, King, Defender of the Faith, &c.*

THOS. GAGE.

By his Excellency's command,
THOS. FLUCKER, Secry.

GOD save the KING.

2. An Account of the Powder Scare

Early in the morning on Thursday, 1 September, the British troops seized gunpowder stored by some Massachusetts farmers near Cambridge. A crowd soon gathered and demanded the resignation of the Mandamus Council members (a group appointed by Gage after the arrival of the Massachusetts Government Act in early August 1774). When the crowd threatened violence, the Boston Committee of Correspondence, under the leadership of Joseph Warren, spoke and calmed the people. Seven men resigned their positions on the Mandamus Council that day, Judge Danforth one of them. Others resigned in the following days as agitation for resignations increased.

The *Boston Evening-Post* 5 September 1774, ran a long account of the powder seizure and the patriot response:

The Committee of Boston sent off an express . . . to advise their brethren of Salem of what they apprehended was coming against them, who received their message with great politeness, and returned an answer purporting their readiness to receive any attack they might be exposed to for acting in pursuance to the laws and interest of their country as became Men & Christians.

From these several hostile appearances the County of Middlesex took the alarm, and on Thursday evening began to collect in large bodies with their arms, provisions and ammunition, determining by some means to give a check to a power which so openly threatned their destruction, and in such a clandestine manner robb'd them of the means of their defense. And on Friday morning some thousands of them had advanced to Cambridge, armed only with sticks, as they had left their fire arms, &c. at some distance behind them. . . .

On perceiving the concourse on Friday morning, the Committee of Cambridge sent express to Charlestown, who communicated the intelligence to Boston, and their respective committees proceeded to Cambridge without delay. When the first of the Boston Committee came up, they found thousands of People assembled before the Court House, and Judge Danforth standing on the steps speaking to the Body. . . .

3. Gage's Proclamation Proroguing the General Court

On 28 September 1774, Gage presented a proclamation proroguing the General Court. It was published in the *Massachusetts Gazette and Boston Post-Boy*, 3 October 1774:

PROVINCE OF MASSACHUSETTS-BAY.
By the Governor.
A PROCLAMATION

WHEREAS on the first Day of *September* Instant, I thought for to issue Writs, for calling a Great and General Court, or Assembly, to be convened and held at Salem, in the County of Essex, on the Fifth Day of October next; And whereas from the many Tumults and Disorders which have since taken place, the extraordinary Resolves which have been passed in many of the Counties, the Instructions given by the Town of Boston, and some other Towns, to their Representatives, and the present disorder'd, and unhappy State of the Province, it appears to me highly inexpedient that a Great and General Court should be convened, at the Time aforesaid; but that a Session, at some more distant Day, will best tend to promote his Majesty's Service, and the good of the Province.

I HAVE therefore thought fit, to declare my Intentio[n]s, not to meet the said General-Court at Salem, on the said Fifth Day of October next. And I do hereby excuse and discharge, all such Persons as have been, or may be elected and deputed Representatives to serve at the same, from giving their Attendance; any Thing in the aforesaid Writs contained to the contrary notwithstanding; whereof all concerned are to take Notice and govern themselves accordingly.

And the Sheriffs of the several Counties, their under Sheriffs, or Deputies, and the Constables of the several Towns within the same, are commanded to cause this Proclamation, to be forthwith published and posted within their Precincts.

G I V E N *at Boston, the Twenty-eighth Day of* September 1774, *in the Fourteenth Year of the Reign of our sovereign* LORD, GEORGE *the Third, by the Grace of* GOD, *of Great-Britain, France and Ireland,* KING, *Defender of the Faith, &c.*

By His Excellency's Command,
   THO's FLUCKER, Sec'ry.

Tho's Gage

GOD *Save the* KING.

Bibliography

Akers, Charles W. *The Divine Politician: Samuel Cooper and the American Revolution.* Boston: Northeastern University Press, 1982.
Adams, John. *Diary and Autobiography of John Adams.* Edited by L. H. Butterfield et al. 4 vols. Cambridge: Harvard University Press, 1961–66.
Adams, Thomas R. *American Independence: The Growth of an Idea. A Bibliographic Study of the American Political Pamphlets Printed Between 1764 and 1776, Dealing with the Dispute Between Britain and Her Colonies.* Providence: Brown University Press, 1965.
Andrews, John. *Letters of John Andrews, Esq., of Boston, 1772–1776.* Edited by Winthrop Sargent. Cambridge, Mass.: John Wilson & Sons, 1866.
Bailyn, Bernard. *The Ideological Origins of the American Revolution.* Cambridge: Harvard University Press, 1967. (All Bailyn quotations in notes to the text refer to this work, unless specifically designated to the volume below.)
———. *The Ordeal of Thomas Hutchinson.* Cambridge: Harvard University Press, 1974.
Baldwin, Alice M. *The New England Clergy and the American Revolution.* Durham, N.C.: Duke University Press, 1928.
Becker, Carl Lotus. *The History of Political Parties in the Province of New York, 1760–1776.* 1909. Reprint. Madison: University of Wisconsin Press, 1968.
Bercovitch, Sacvan. *The American Jeremiad.* Madison: University of Wisconsin Press, 1978.
———. *The Puritan Origins of the American Self.* New Haven: Yale University Press, 1975.
Berry, Lloyd E., ed. *The Geneva Bible: A Facsimile of the 1560 Edition.* Madison: University of Wisconsin Press, 1969.
The New Bible Dictionary. Edited by J. D. Douglas. Grand Rapids, Mich.: William B. Eerdmans, 1962.
Boatner, Mark Mayo, III. *Encyclopedia of the American Revolution.* New York: David McKay, 1966.
"The Boston Ministers: A Ballad [1774]." *New England Historical and Genealogical Register* 13 (1859): 131–33.
Bowman, J. R. "A Bibliography of *The First Book of the American Chronicles of the Times, 1774–1775.*" *American Literature* 1 (1929): 68–74.
Brewer's Dictionary of Phrase and Fable. Rev. ed. 1952. Reprint. New York: Harper and Bros., n.d.
Bridenbaugh, Carl. *Mitre and Sceptre: Transatlantic Faiths, Ideas, Personalities, and Politics, 1689–1775.* New York: Oxford University Press, 1962.
Brown, Robert E. *Middle-Class Democracy and the Revolution in Massachusetts, 1691–1790.* Ithaca: Cornell University Press, 1955.

Butler, Jon. "The Future of American Religious History: Prospectus, Agenda, Transatlantic *Problematique*." *William and Mary Quarterly*, 3d ser., 42 (1985): 167–83.

Cabeen, Francis von A. "The Society of the Sons of St. Tammany of Philadelphia." *Pennsylvania Magazine of History and Biography* 25 (1901): 433–51; 26 (1902): 7–24, 207–23, 355–47, 443–63.

Capp, Bernard. "The Political Dimension of Apocalyptic Thought." *The Apocalypse in English Renaissance Thought and Literature: Patterns, Antecedents and Repercussions*. Edited by C. A. Patrides and Joseph Wittreich. Manchester: Manchester University Press, 1984.

The Century Dictionary and Cyclopedia. Rev. ed. 12 vols. 1889. Reprint. New York: Century, 1913.

Christie, Ian R. and Benjamin W. Labaree. *Empire or Independence, 1760–1776: A British-American Dialogue on the Coming of the American Revolution*. 1976. Reprint. New York: W. W. Norton, 1977.

Colbourn, H. Trevor. *The Lamp of Experience: Whig History and the Intellectual Origins of the American Revolution*. 1965. Reprint. New York: W. W. Norton, 1974.

Crary, Catherine Snell. "The Tory and the Spy: The Double Life of James Rivington." *William and Mary Quarterly*, 3d ser., 16 (1959): 61–72.

Dallett, Francis James, Jr. "John Leacock and *The Fall of British Tyranny*." *Pennsylvania Magazine of History and Biography* 78 (1954): 456–75.

Damon, S. Foster. *Yankee Doodle*. Providence: Brown University Press, 1959.

Davidson, James West. *The Logic of Millennial Thought: Eighteenth-Century New England*. New Haven: Yale University Press, 1977.

Davidson, Philip. *Propaganda and the American Revolution, 1763–1783*. Chapel Hill: University of North Carolina Press, 1941.

Deane, Charles. "'Protesters' Against the Solemn League and Covenant." *Proceedings of the Massachusetts Historical Society* 11 (1870): 392–95.

Dictionary of American Biography. Edited by Allen Johnson. 10 vols. New York: Charles Scribner's Sons, 1928–36.

Dictionary of American English on Historical Principles. Edited by William A. Craigie and James Hulbert et al. 4 vols. Chicago: University of Chicago Press, 1942.

A *Dictionary of American Proverbs and Proverbial Phrases*. Edited by B. J. Whiting and Archie Taylor. Cambridge: Harvard University Press, 1598.

Dictionary of Americanisms on Historical Principles. Edited by Mitford M. Mathews. 3 vols. Chicago: University of Chicago Press, 1951.

Dictionary of National Biography. Edited by Leslie Stephen and Sidney Lee et al. 66 vols. [London]: Oxford University Press, 1885–1900.

Dictionary of Philosophy and Psychology. Edited by James Mark Baldwin. 3 vols. New York: Macmillan, 1905.

A *Dictionary of the English Language*. By Samuel Johnson. 2 vols. London: W. Strahan, 1755.

Donnelly, Lucy M. "The Celebrated Mrs. Macaulay." *William and Mary Quarterly*, 3d ser., 6 (1949): 190–202.

Dunlap, William. *A History of the American Theatre*. New York: Harper, 1832.

Endy, Melvin B., Jr. "Just War, Holy War, and Millennialism in Revolutionary America." *William and Mary Quarterly*, 3d ser., 42 (1985) : 3–25.

Evans, Emory G. *Thomas Nelson of Yorktown: Revolutionary Virginian*. Charlottesville, Va.: University Press of Virginia for the Colonial Williamsburg Foundation, 1975.

Field, Edward, ed. *The State of Rhode Island and Providence Plantations at the End of the Century.* 2 vols. Boston: Mason Publishing, 1902.

Firth, Katharine R. *The Apocalyptic Tradition in Reformation Britain, 1530–1645.* Oxford: Oxford University Press, 1979.

Ford, Paul Leicester, ed. *The New England Primer.* N.d. Reprint. New York: Columbia Teachers College, 1962.

———. *Some Notes towards an Essay on the Beginnings of American Dramatic Literature, 1606–1789.* 25 copies printed. New York: Printed for the author, 1893.

Franklin, Benjamin. *The Papers of Benjamin Franklin.* Edited by Leonard W. Labaree et al. New Haven: Yale UP, 1959–.

———. *The Writings of Benjamin Franklin.* Edited by Albert Henry Smyth. 10 vols. New York: Macmillan, 1907.

Fraser, Antonia. *Cromwell: The Lord Protector.* New York: Alfred A. Knopf, 1973.

Frothingham, Richard. "Address 'To Governor Hutchinson' and the 'Solemn League and Covenant.'" *Proceedings of the Massachusetts Historical Society* 12 (1871) : 43–48.

Galvin, John R. *Three Men of Boston.* New York: Crowell, 1976.

Garrett, Clarke. *Respectable Folly: Millenarians and the French Revolution in France and England.* Baltimore: Johns Hopkins University Press, 1975.

Granger, Bruce Ingham. *Political Satire in the American Revolution.* Ithaca: Cornell University Press, 1960.

Griffin, Edward M. *Old Brick: Charles Chauncy of Boston, 1705–1787.* Minneapolis: University of Minnesota Press, 1980.

Hall, David D. *The Faithful Shepherd: A History of the New England Ministry in the Seventeenth Century.* Chapel Hill: University of North Carolina Press for the Institute of Early American History and Culture, 1972.

Harper's Latin Dictionary. Edited by E. A. Andrews. Rev. ed. by Charlton T. Lewis and Charles Short. New York: American Books, 1907.

Harrison, J. F. C. *The Second Coming: Popular Millenarianism, 1780–1850.* London: Routledge and Kegan Paul, 1979.

Hastings, George Everett. *The Life and Works of Francis Hopkinson.* Chicago: University of Chicago Press, 1926.

Hatch, Nathan O. *The Sacred Cause of Liberty: Republican Thought and the Millennium in Revolutionary New England.* New Haven: Yale University Press, 1977.

Hay, Robert P. "The Liberty Tree: A Symbol for American Patriots." *Quarterly Journal of Speech* 55 (1969): 414–24.

Heimert, Alan. *Religion and the American Mind.* Cambridge: Harvard University Press, 1966.

Hildeburn, Charles R. *A Century of Printing: The Issues of the Press in Pennsylvania, 1685–1784.* Philadelphia: Matlack and Harvey, 1886.

Hill, Christopher. *Antichrist in Seventeenth-Century England.* London: Oxford University Press, 1971.

———. *God's Englishman: Oliver Cromwell and the English Revolution.* New York: Dial Press, 1970.

———. *The World Turned Upside Down: Radical Ideas during the English Revolution.* New York: Viking Press, 1972.

Hopkinson, Francis. *The Miscellaneous Essays and Occasional Writings of Francis Hopkinson.* 3 vols. Philadelphia: T. Dobson, 1792.

Humphreys, David. *The Miscellaneous Works of David Humphreys.* 1804. Edited by William Bottorff. Reprint. Gainesville, Fla.: Scholars' Facsimiles and Reprints, 1968.

Hutcheon, Linda. *A Theory of Parody: The Teachings of Twentieth-Century Art Forms.* New York: Methuen, 1985.

Jackson, M. Katherine. *Outlines of the Literary History of Colonial Pennsylvania.* 1907. Reprint. New York: AMS Press, 1966.

Jefferson, Thomas. *The Papers of Thomas Jefferson.* Edited by Julien P. Boyd et al. Princeton: Princeton University Press, 1950–.

Jensen, Merrill. *The Founding of a Nation: The History of the American Revolution, 1763–1776.* New York: Oxford University Press, 1968.

The Journals of Each Provincial Congress of Massachusetts in 1774 and 1775. Edited by William Lincoln. Boston: Dutton and Wentworth, 1838. (Cited in notes as *Prov. Jnls.*)

Karsten, Peter. *Patriot Heroes in England and America: Political Symbolism and Changing Values over Three Centuries.* Madison: University of Wisconsin Press, 1979.

Korshin, Paul. "Queuing and Waiting: The Apocalypse in England, 1660–1750." *The Apocalypse in English Renaissance Thought and Literature: Patterns, Antecedents and Repercussions.* Edited by C. A. Patrides and Joseph Wittreich. Manchester: Manchester University Press, 1984.

———. *Typologies in England, 1650–1820.* Princeton: Princeton University Press, 1982.

Labaree, Benjamin W. *America's Nation-Time: 1607–1789.* 1972. Reprint. New York: W. W. Norton, 1976.

Lane, William C. "The Rebellion of 1766 in Harvard College." *Publications of the Colonial Society of Massachusetts* 9 (1905): 33–59.

Launitz-Schurer, Leopold S., Jr. *Loyal Whigs and Revolutionaries: The Making of the Revolution in New York, 1765–1776.* New York: New York University Press, 1980.

Lemay, J. A. Leo. "The American Origins of 'Yankee Doodle.'" *William and Mary Quarterly,* 3d ser., 33 (1976): 435–64.

———. "The Frontiersman from Lout to Hero: Notes on the Significance of the Comparative Method and the Stage Theory in Early American Literature and Culture." *Proceedings of the American Antiquarian Society* 88 (1979): 187–223.

Leventhal, Herbert. *In the Shadow of the Enlightenment: Occultism and Renaissance Science in Eighteenth-Century America.* New York: New York University Press, 1976.

McCarter, Peter Kyle. "Mother Carey's Jacobin Chickens." *Early American Literature* 14 (1979): 163–73.

Man, Myth, & Magic: An Illustrated Encyclopedia of the Supernatural. Edited by Richard Cavendish. 24 vols. New York: Marshall Cavendish Corp., 1970.

Matthews, Albert C. "The Book of America." *Proceedings of the Massachusetts Historical Society* 62 (1930): 171–97.

———. "Brother Jonathan." *Publications of the Colonial Society of Massachusetts* 7 (1902): 94–125.

———. "The Solemn League and Covenant, 1774." *Publications of the Colonial Society of Massachusetts* 18 (1916): 103–22.

May, Henry F. *The Enlightenment in America.* Oxford: Oxford University Press, 1976.

Mays, David M., ed. *The Disappointment, or, the Force of Credulity [1767].* Gainesville: University Press of Florida, 1976.

The Memorial History of Boston. Edited by Justin Winsor. 4 vols. Boston: James R. Osgood, 1881. (Cited in text as *Winsor.*)

Mencken, H. L. *The American Language: An Inquiry into the Development of English in the United States*. 1919. Reprint. New York: Alfred A. Knopf, 1962.

Miller, John C. *Sam Adams: Pioneer in Propaganda*. Boston: Little, Brown, 1936.

Moore, Frank. *Songs and Ballads of the American Revolution*. 1855. Reprint. New York: Hurst, 1904.

Moses, Montrose J. *The American Dramatist*. Boston: Little, Brown, 1917.

Mulford [Micklus], Carla. "John Leacock's *A New Song, On the Repeal of the Stamp-Act*." *Early American Literature* 15 (1980): 188–93.

Oliver, Peter. *Peter Oliver's Origin & Progress of the American Rebellion: A Tory View [1781]*. Edited by Douglass Adair and John A. Schutz. San Marino, Calif.: Huntington Library, 1963.

Oppenheim, Samuel. "The Chapters of Isaac the Scribe: A Bibliographical Rarity, New York, 1772." *Publications of the American Jewish Historical Society* 22 (1914): 39–51.

The Oxford English Dictionary. Edited by James A. H. Murray et al. 13 vols. 1884–1928. Reprint. Oxford: Oxford University Press, 1933.

A Supplement to the Oxford English Dictionary. 2 vols. Oxford: Clarendon Press, 1972.

Patrides, C. A. "'Something like Prophetick strain': Apocalyptic Configurations in Milton." *The Apocalypse in English Renaissance Thought and Literature: Patterns, Antecedents and Repercussions*. Edited by C. A. Patrides and Joseph Wittreich. Manchester: Manchester University Press, 1984.

Patterson, Stephen E. *Political Parties in Revolutionary Massachusetts*. Madison: University of Wisconsin Press, 1973.

Philadelphia: Three Centuries of American Art. Philadelphia: Philadelphia Museum of Art, 1976.

Philbrick, Norman O. *Trumpets Sounding: Propaganda Plays of the American Revolution*. New York: Benjamin Blom, 1972.

Rees, James. *The Dramatic Authors of America*. Philadelphia: G. B. Zieber, 1845.

Rose, Margaret A. *Parody//Meta-Fiction: An Analysis of Parody as a Critical Mirror to the Writing and Reception of Fiction*. London: Croom Helm, 1979.

Rubel, Margaret Mary. *Savage and Barbarian: Historical Attitudes in the Criticism of Homer and Ossian in Britain, 1760–1800*. Amsterdam: Holland Publishing, 1978.

Sabin, Joseph. *Bibliotheca Americana: A Dictionary of Books Relating to America*. New York: Bibliographical Society of America, 1878.

Schlesinger, Arthur M. "Liberty Tree: A Genealogy." *New England Quarterly*, 35 (1962): 435–58.

―――― *Prelude to Independence: The Newspaper War on Britain, 1764–1776*. New York: Alfred A. Knopf, 1958.

Seilhamer, George O. *History of the American Theatre: During the Revolution and After*. Philadelphia: Globe Printing, 1889.

Shipton, Clifford. *Sibley's Harvard Graduates: Biographical Sketches of Those Who Attended Harvard College*. Vols. 4–16. Boston: Harvard University Press and Mass. Historical Society, 1932–1972.

Simms, P. Marion. *The Bible in America*. New York: Wilson-Erickson, 1936.

Slotkin, Richard. *Regeneration through Violence: The Mythology of the American Frontier, 1600–1860*. Middletown, Conn.: Wesleyan University Press, 1973.

Sprague, William B. *Annals of the American Pulpit*. 12 vols. New York: Robert Carter and Bros., 1857.

Stein, Stephen J. "Transatlantic Expressions: Apocalyptic in Early New England." *The Apocalypse in English Renaissance Thought and Literature: Patterns, Antecedents and Repercussions.* Edited by C. A. Patrides and Joseph Wittreich. Manchester: Manchester University Press, 1984.

Stokes, Anson Phelps. *Memorials of Eminent Yale Men.* 2 vols. New Haven: Yale University Press, 1914.

Teeter, Dwight L. "Benjamin Towne: The Precarious Career of a Persistent Printer." *Pennsylvania Magazine of History and Biography* 89 (1965): 316–30.

Tuckerman, Frederick. "The Diary of Samuel Cooper, 1775–1776." *American Historical Review* 6 (1901): 301–41.

———. "Letters of Samuel Cooper to Thomas Pownall, 1769–1777." *American Historical Review* 8 (1903): 301–30.

Tyler, Moses Coit. *The Literary History of the American Revolution, 1763–1783.* 2 vols. 1897. Reprint. New York: Barnes and Noble, 1941.

Van Doren, Carl. *Benjamin Franklin.* New York: Viking, 1938.

Virga, Patricia H. *The American Opera to 1790.* Ann Arbor: UMI Research Press, 1982.

Walpole, Horace. *Horace Walpole's Correspondence with Sir Horace Mann. Vol 1. The Yale Edition of Horace Walpole's Correspondence.* Vol. 17. Edited by W. S. Lewis. New Haven: Yale University Press, 1954.

Watson, John Fanning. *Annals of Philadelphia, and Pennsylvania, in the Olden Time being a Collection of Memoirs, Anecdotes, and Incidents of the City and Its Inhabitants, and of the Earliest Settlements of the Inland Part of Pennsylvania.* Philadelphia: Published for the author, 1850.

Webster's Biographical Dictionary. Rev. ed. Springfield, Mass.: G. and C. Merriam, 1976.

Wegelin, Oscar. *Early American Plays, 1714–1830.* New York: Dunlap Society, 1900.

Wood, Gordon S. *The Creation of the American Republic, 1776–1787.* Chapel Hill: University of North Carolina Press for the Institute of Early American History and Culture, 1969.

Woodress, James. *A Yankee's Odyssey: The Life of Joel Barlow.* 1958. Reprint. New York: Greenwood Press, 1968.

Young, Alfred F. "English Plebian Culture and Eighteenth-Century American Radicalism." *The Origins of Anglo-American Radicalism.* Edited by Margaret Jacob and James Jacob. London: Allen and Unwin, 1984.

Index

The characters of *The First Book of the American Chronicles of the Times* are listed in Appendix B: List of Characters.

Abbot, Robert, 100 n.30
Adams, John, 19, 101 n.5; on colonial right to self-government, 90–91 n.12; on Cooper's preaching, 21–22; on Cromwell, 32–33, 34, 42 n.46; delegate to First Continental Congress, 20, 86n.39, 88n.56, 102n.8; on Hancock, 44n.69; Hutchinson's fear of, 21; informed of powder scare, 88n.56; on tea dumping, 91–92n.17; on Whately letters, 21–22, 44n.69
Adams, Samuel, 19, 41n.32, 101n.5; British urged to plunder, 24; delegate to First Continental Congress, 20, 86n.39, 102n.8; Hutchinson's fear of, 21; as Jedediah the scribe, 20, 85n.24
Adams, Thomas R., 48n.130, 83n.12
Administration of Justice Act (1774), 105n.18. *See also* Coercive Acts
Akers, Charles, 42nn. 35, 36, 37, and 45; 43nn. 51, 53, 54, and 55; 44n.71
Allegory, biblical, 28
Allen, Ethan, 108
American Philosophical Society, 13, 15, 40n.18, 41nn. 21 and 23, 81, 106n.42
Aminadab, 23, 26, 87n.43. *See also* Cooper, William
Anderson, John: *Book of the Chronicles of His Royal Highness*, 29
Andrews, John: annoyed by British insults, 86n.36, 93n.33; celebrated Israel Putnam, 94n.46; commended response to powder scare, 87n.50, 94n.46; disliked Solemn League, 24, 43n.57; shocked at British treatment of deserters, 102n.12
Andros, Edmund, 19, 96nn. 30 and 31; as Balaam the wizard, 19, 96nn. 30 and 31
Anglican church, 31, 105nn. 21 and 22
Anglicanism, 97n.37

Anne Arundel County Committee of Observation, 101n.2
Apocalypse, 31, 32, 45n.91, 46n.97
Apocalyptic, 12, 35, 36, 45nn. 91 and 93, 46n.97, 81
Auchmuty, Robert, 83n.12

Bailyn, Bernard, 12, 18, 39n.8, 41n.28, 44n.81, 45nn. 88 and 89, 97n.2
Bakhtin, Mikhail, 47n.122
Baldwin, Alice M., 42n.35, 43n.59, 84n.19, 93n.36
Barlow, Joel, 44–45n.82
Barrington, Lord William, 83n.10
Battle of Louisburg. *See* French and Indian War
Battle of Marston Moor, 99nn. 21 and 27
Becker, Carl L., 97nn. 1 and 2, 98n.4
Belcher, Jonathan, 21, 42n.44
Bell, Robert, 44n.79
Bercovitch, Sacvan, 46nn. 97 and 98, 97n.37
Bernard, Francis, 19, 83n.10; Bernardites, 19
Berry, Lloyd E., 43n.49, 81–82
Beverley, Robert, 41n.30
Bible, Apocrypha in, 81. Books of: Acts, 24, 84n.14, 93n.29, 98n.8, 99n.24, 102n.9; Amos, 95n.5; 1 Chronicles, 17, 85nn.27 and 31, 87nn. 48 and 49, 88nn. 55, 57, and 58; 2 Chronicles, 86n.42, 88n.53, 101n.7; 2 Corinthians, 97n.35; Daniel, 17, 31, 82n.4, 89n.74, 93n.30, 105n.23; Deuteronomy, 26, 83n.7, 84n.21, 85nn. 25 and 26, 88nn. 52 and 54, 90n.9, 92n.20, 93nn. 36 and 37, 94nn. 43 and 47, 95n.8, 96n.29, 103n.1, 104n.7, 106nn. 37, 38, 39, 40, 41, and 43; 107nn. 45, 46, 47, 48, and

123

49; Ecclesiastes, 93n.32, 94–95n.3, 95nn. 9 and 10, 106n.29, 109; Esther, 30, 83n.8, 99n.22; Exodus, 89n.73, 106n.32; Ezekiel, 86n.34, 94n.41; Ezra, 89n.74; Genesis, 29, 87n.48, 88n.60, 96n.24, 104n.13, 109; Hebrews, 84n.21; Isaiah, 101n.1, 103n.2, 106nn. 31 and 34; Jeremiah, 86n.42, 87n.44, 93–94n.39, 103n.2, 106n.34; Job, 84n.18, 89n.74, 90n.7; Jonah, 84n.22; Joshua, 86n.38, 89n.73; Judges, 83n.7, 88n.62, 102n.12, 104n.7; 1 Kings, 81, 91nn. 14 and 15, 101n.7, 104nn. 5, 6, and 13, 109; 2 Kings, 86n.42, 96n.23; Luke, 88n.63, 91n.13, 109; Mark, 91n.13, 94n.48, 99n.19, 107n.44, 109; Matthew, 17, 82n.3, 91n.13, 98n.5, 99n.19, 103nn. 2 and 17, 105n.20, 109; Micah, 99n.25; Nehemiah, 84n.22, 89n.68; Numbers, 84n.21, 88n.54, 90n.2, 95nn. 7 and 17, 96n.31, 103n.18, 106n.43, 109; Obadiah, 85n.33, 96n.26; 2 Peter, 103n.18; Proverbs, 82, 94nn. 1 and 2, 96nn. 27 and 28; Psalms, 90nn. 3 and 8, 92nn. 19, 22, 23, and 24; 93n.35, 95nn. 7, 11, 19, 20, 21, and 22; 96n.25, 99n.20, 105n.24, 106nn. 30, 35, and 36; 109; Revelation, 21, 31, 33, 81, 95n.16, 102n.13, 105n.23; Romans, 93n.31; 1 Samuel, 83n.7, 88n.53, 95n.15, 96n.32, 97nn. 34, 36, and 37; 2 Samuel, 28, 84n.22, 85n.24, 87n.47, 88n.56, 90n.4, 93n.38; 1 Timothy, 87n.46, 95n.12; 2 Timothy, 95n.13, 103n.2. See also Geneva Bible; King James Bible

Bible hoax, 29, 45n.84

Blake, Robert, 99nn.15, 16, and 18; 100n.30

Boatner, Mark Mayo, III, 44n.74

Bolingbroke, Henry St. John, Viscount, 92–93n.27

Bolton, Thomas, 22, 43n.51

"Book of America," 29, 44n.82

"Book of Harvard," 29, 44n.82

Boston Committee of Correspondence. See Committee(s) of Correspondence

Boston Committee of Safety, 101n.4

Boston Evening-Post, 86n.41, 114

Boston Gazette, 21, 24, 83n.10, 92n.21, 102n.8

Boston massacre, 26

Boston Ministers (1774), 22, 25, 43n.50

Boston Port Bill (1774), 83n.6, 84–85n.23, 92n.26. See also Coercive Acts

Boston Post-Boy, 102n.8, 115

Boston Tea Party, 16, 82n.5, 83n.8, 84n.20, 91–92n.17

Bostwick, Nuel: *First Book of Chronicles*, 30, 45n.87

Bowdoin, James, 24, 86n.39

Bowman, J. R., 12, 38, 39n.5, 48n.130

Boyle, Roger, Baron Broghill, 100n.30

Braddock, Gen. Edward, 43n.60, 92nn. 18 and 20

Bradshaw, John, 101n.31

Brattle, William, 44n.69, 87n.50, 89–90n.75

Brattle Street Church, 11, 17, 20, 21; attended by Andrews, 24; attended by Hancock, 26; merchant audience of, 21, 23, 24, 26; scene of patriot meetings, 21

Bremer, Francis J., 46n.101

Bridenbaugh, Carl, 97n.2, 105n.21

British East India Tea Company, 16, 82n.2

Brown, Robert E., 88n.56, 90n.6, 92n.24, 94n.40, 101n.33

Burke, Edmund, 92n.26

Burnet, Bp. Thomas, 98n.9

Bute, John Stuart, third Earl of, 13, 19, 92–93n.27, 108, 109

Butler, Jon, 47n.113

Cabeen, Francis von A., 91n.17

Cadwalader, John, 41n.22

Caleb, 88n.54, 94n.47. See also Warren, Joseph

Cambridge Platonists, 31

Camisards, 31

Capp, Bernard, 45n.91, 46n.100

Carey, Mother or Sister: Aminadab and Jedediah meet, 26; attracts Jedediah, 20; and chickens, 44n.73, 96–97n.33, 102n.15; Dorcas Griffiths as, 27; Elizabeth Cary as, 96–97n.33; as local witch, 17, 26, 35; Obadiah's charmer, 17, 26

Carolus King of Hispania (Charles V), 19, 104n.11

Cary, Elizabeth, 96–97n.33

Catechisms, 30

Catholicism, 11, 18, 97n.37, 98n.13

Catholics, 81, 98nn. 12 and 13, 102n.11,

104n.8; domination by, 45n.93; population of, in Quebec, 91n.16, 102n.11; and scholasticism, 103nn. 16 and 20. See also Roman Catholic Church

Chandler, Thomas B., 97nn. 1 and 2

"Chapters of Isaac the Scribe," 29, 30, 45nn.83 and 86

Charles I, 85n.29, 92n.25, 98nn. 7 and 13, 99n.23, 100n.30, 101n.31

Charles II, 28, 46n.100, 98–99n.14, 104n.9

Charter of 1629, Massachusetts, 18, 92n.24, 98n.7, 105n.18

Charter of 1691, Massachusetts, 18, 98n.7, 105n.18

Chauncy, Charles, 17, 87n.44; active as Whig patriot, 42n.35; believed in civil millennium, 25; jeremiads of, 24–25, 43n.60; as Jeremiah, 17, 24–25, 87n.44; pastor of First Church, 21, 24; refused to read proclamations, 84n.19; spoke of deserved deliverance of colonists, 25

Christ Church, 14, 16

Christie, Ian R., 82n.3, 84n.20, 85n.30, 91n.16

Chronicle of the Kings of England, 29, 44n.79

Church, Benjamin, 20, 88n.56

Church of England, 31, 105nn. 21 and 22

Coercive Acts, 16, 108; affected colonial right to self-government, 105n.18; colonial resolves in response to, 90–91n.12; Cooper brothers opposed, 24; Declaration of Colonial Rights and Grievances in response to, 90–91n.12; Mansfield fostered, through Parliament, 93n.28; North blamed for, by colonists, 106n.28

Colbourn, H. Trevor, 28, 41n.25, 44n.78, 47nn. 106, 107, and 108

Colden, Cadwallader, 41n.30

Committee(s) of Correspondence, 84–85n.23, 86n.37, 105n.21, 114–15; in Boston, 23, 24, 26, 27, 84–85n.23, 85n.29, 86n.41, 114–15

Committee of Observation, Anne Arundel County, 101n.2

Committee of Safety, Boston, 101n.4

Commonwealth, 33, 36, 98n.10

Constitutional Gazette (New York), 12–13

Continental Association, 90–91n.12

Convention Parliament (1660), 99n.23

Coombe, Thomas, 15, 41n.23

Cooper, Miles, 19, 97nn. 1 and 2; Cooperites, 19

Cooper, Samuel, 11, 17; as arresting preacher, 20, 21, 23; attacked in *Boston Ministers* and Bolton's *Oration*, 22; called "Silver-Tongued Sam," 22, 43n.49; chief confidant of Franklin on colonial affairs, 21, 23; considered prompter of brother William, 24; credited with political essays, 21; Hutchinson feared, 21; as influential politician, 20–21; as Jedediah the priest, 17, 20–23, 85n.24, 94n.44; offered Harvard College presidency, 23; Peter Oliver denigrated, 23; popular with women, 23, 26; used parsonage for secret meetings, 21; Whig ideology in sermons of, 21–22, 42n.35

Cooper, Rev. William (father of Samuel and William), 94n.44; as Eliphalet, 94n.44

Cooper, William, 17, 23–24, 87n.43; as Aminadab, 17, 23–24, 87n.43

Coote, Sir Charles, Earl of Mountrath, 100n.30

Crary, Catherine S., 98n.3

Cromwell, Oliver, 11, 17, 18, 19, 32–36, 109; army of, 100n.30; blamed for British standing army, 32, 47n.106; body disinterred, 99n.23; compact of, called Solemn League and Covenant, 85n.29; as Lord Protector, 97n.39, 98nn. 10, 11, and 12; in mummers' plays, 36, 48n.126; navigation under, 99nn. 15, 16, 17, and 18; in plebian culture, 34, 36, 48n.126; as second Christ, 32–34; significance to eighteenth-century millenarianism, 31, 32–34

Cushing, Thomas, 19; delegate to First Continental Congress, 20, 86n.39, 102n.8; Franklin informed, of having been dishonored, 84nn.15 and 16; Franklin sent Whately letters to, 22, 42n.40, 83–84n.12, 101n.4; newspaper urged plundering of, 24; patriot activities of, 101n.4

Daggett, Naphtali, 44–45n.82

Dallett, Francis James, Jr., 13, 40nn. 13 and 18

Damon, S. Foster, 87–88n.51

Danforth, Judge Samuel, 87n.50, 90n.6, 114–15
Dartmouth, William Legge, second Earl of, 82n.3, 87n.50
Dartmouth (ship), 82n.2, 85n.26
Davidson, James West, 39–40n.8, 47nn.114, 115, and 116
Davidson, Philip, 39–40n.8, 44nn. 81 and 82, 45nn. 86 and 88
Deane, Charles, 85n.29
Declaration of Colonial Rights and Grievances, 90–91n.12
Deism, 30
Deistic, 11, 37
Desborough, John, 100n.30
Dick, James, 19, 101n.2
Dickinson, John, 92n.21
Disappointment, 13, 40n.11
Dixwell, John, 32
Donnelly, Lucy M., 47n.107
Dryden, John: *Absalom and Achitophel*, 28
Dunlap, William, 13, 40n.12
Dunmore, John Murray, fourth Earl of, 108
Dunning, John, 84n.14

East India Tea Company, 16, 82n.2
Edwards, Jonathan, 25, 33
Eliot, Ephraim, 42n.43
Eliot, John, 41n.30
Endy, Melvin B., Jr., 46n.97, 47n.113
English Revolution, 32, 46n.100
Evans, Charles, 29, 38–39, 45n.86
Evans, Emory G., 103n.22
Ewer, Isaac, 100n.30

Fairfax, Ferdinando, 99n.26, 100n.30
First Church, 24
First Continental Congress, 17, 20, 38, 86nn.39, 40, and 41; 90–91n.12, 98nn.4 and 7, 101n.3, 102n.8, 106n.27
Firth, Katharine R., 45, 81
Fleetwood, Charles, 100n.30
Flucker, Thomas, 114, 116
Ford, Paul Leicester, 13, 40n.12, 105–6n.25
Forrest, Thomas, 13, 40n.11
Fox, Charles James, 92n.26
Franklin, Benjamin, 42n.42, 44n.66; advised moderation before resistance, 36, 83n.8; confided in Samuel Cooper, 21, 23; consulted by Pitt, 104n.4; his correspondence with Jane Mecom, 25, 84n.17; denounced by Wedderburn, 83n.9, 84nn.13, 14, 15, and 16; 105n.15; his family relationship with Leacock, 15, 29, 101n.31, 106n.42; as folk hero, 11, 35; as Mordecai, 16, 19, 30, 83n.8; pretended to absolve king of responsibility, 83n.8; represented Massachusetts Assembly in Privy Council, 83n.9; secured Whately letters, 22, 83–84n.12; wrote Bible hoaxes, 29, 45n.84. Works: *Account of New Invented Fireplaces*, 106n.42; *Causes and Cures of Smoky Chimneys*, 106n.42; *Description of a New Stove*, 106n.42; *Edict by the King of Prussia*, 83n.8; "Parable Against Persecution," 29; "Parable on Brotherly Love," 29; *Rules by Which a Great Empire May be Reduced*, 83n.8
Fraser, Antonia, 97n.39, 98–99n.14, 99nn. 15, 16, and 18; 100n.29
French and Indian War, 17, 22, 27, 92nn. 18 and 20; Battle of Louisburg in, 27, 87–88n.51, 102n.8, 104n.9
French Prophets (Camisards), 31
Friendly Address to All Reasonable Americans, 97n.2
Frothingham, Richard, 85n.29

Gage, Thomas, 13, 17, 106n.27, 108; as commander of British forces, 20, 35, 84n.19, 94n.40, 102n.12; dissolved General Court (1774), 92n.24, 99–100n.28; Hancock's dislike of, 44n.69; informed of backcountry alliance, 90–91n.12; issued proclamations, 85n.32, 99–100n.28, 113–14, 115–16; powder scare activity of, 86n.41, 89–90n.75; as Thomas the Gageite, 16, 19, 81, 90–91n.12
Galloway, Joseph, 86n.40
Galvin, John R., 82n.2, 83nn. 6 and 10, 84n.20
Garrett, Clarke, 45n.91
Geneva Bible, 43n.49, 81–82, 89n.74
George III, 16, 19, 36, 82n.3, 83nn. 6 and 8, 90–91n.12, 92nn. 24 and 26, 92–93n.27, 106n.27, 109, 113–14, 116; as Rehoboam, 16, 19, 81, 82n.3, 90n.11
Gibbons, Christopher, 100n.30
Glorious Revolution, 98n.7, 105n.18
Goffe, William, 32

Index

Goodman, Roy E., 41n.21
Grand Congress. *See* First Continental Congress
Granger, Bruce I., 12, 19, 39n.7, 41n.33, 44n.82
Graves, Thomas, 14
Great Awakening, 33, 47n.113
Grenville, George, 13, 83–84n.12
Griffin, Edward, 43n.60
Griffiths, Dorcas, 27

Hall, David (printer), 15, 29
Hall, David D., 46n.97
Hammond, Robert, 100n.30
Hancock, John, 17, 22, 85n.33, 96–97n.33; ambivalent about resistance in early 1770s, 26; attended Brattle Street Church, 26; friendship with Dorcas Griffiths, 27; as merchant, 26, 101n.32; newspaper urged plundering of, 24; as Obadiah, 17, 26–27, 85n.33, 96–97n.33; *Oration* of, 26; patriot activities of, 20, 21, 26, 82n.5, 101n.32; shrewdness of, 44n.68; submitted Whately letters, 26, 101n.32
Harrison, J. F. C., 45n.91
Harrison, Thomas, 100n.30
Hastings, George Everett, 12, 39n.4, 40n.9
Hatch, Nathan O., 25, 43n.48, 44nn.64 and 65, 87n.46, 105n.21
Hawley, Major, 44n.69
Hay, Robert P., 92n.25
Hayley (ship), 82n.5
Heimert, Alan, 42n.35, 43n.62, 47n.113
Hewson, John, 100n.30
Hildeburn, Charles R., 13, 40n.12
Hill, Christopher, 46n.100
Hoax, biblical, 29, 45n.84
Holt, John, 29, 30
Hopkins, Stephen: *Fall of Samuel the Squomicutite*, 29
Hopkinson, Francis, 12, 14, 29–30, 45n.85
Horrocks, Rev. James, 97n.2
Hume, David, 47, 103n.21
Humphreys, David, 44n.74
Huske, John, 13
Hutcheon, Linda, 34–35, 45n.90, 47nn.118, 120, 122, and 123; 48n.124
Hutchinson, Thomas, 16, 19, 20, 22, 26, 42n.39, 82n.2, 83nn.9, 10, and 11; 83–84n.12, 85nn. 26 and 29, 90n.1; Hutchinsonians, 19, 83n.11; as Judas the Parasite, 16, 19, 90n.1
Hutchinson or Whately letters, 21, 22, 26, 83–84n.12, 101n.32
Hyde, Edward, Earl of Clarendon, 98n.9

Independent Ledger, 21
Ingenhousz, Jan, 106n.42
Inglis, Charles, 97n.1
Intolerable Acts. *See* Coercive Acts
Ireton, Henry, 100n.30

Jackson, M. Katherine, 12, 39n.3
Jedediah, 19, 20, 23, 26, 35–36, 85n.24, 109. *See also* Adams, Samuel; Cooper, Samuel
Jefferson, Thomas, 47n.106, 101n.31
Jensen, Merrill, 41n.25, 44n.75, 82nn. 2 and 5, 83n.6, 84n.19, 84–85n.23, 85nn. 29 and 30, 86nn. 37, 39, 40, and 41; 87n.50, 88n.56, 89–90n.75, 92n.18, 98n.7, 101n.2, 104n.14, 105n.18
Jeremiad(s), 24, 43n.62, 46n.97
Jeremiah, 18, 19, 20, 26, 41n.32, 87n.44. *See also* Chauncy, Charles
Johnson, Samuel, 34, 47nn.119 and 121, 103n.21
Johnson, Sir William, 43n.60
"Jonathan," 86n.35, 88n.61
Jones, Michael, 100n.30

Karsten, Peter, 48n.127
King James Bible, 29, 81–82
Korshin, Paul J., 31, 45nn. 91 and 94, 46nn. 95, 96, and 100

Labaree, Benjamin W., 82n.3, 84n.20, 85nn. 26 and 30, 90–91n.12, 91n.16, 106n.27
Lambert, John, 99n.27, 100n.30
Lane, William C., 44–45n.82
Lapland witches, 102n.14
Launitz-Schurer, Leopold S., Jr., 97n.2, 98n.3
Lawson, John, 41n.30
Leacock, John, 12–16, 30, 36, 38, 88n.63, 95n.5, 102n.10; activities of, during Revolutionary War, 15; activities of, during Stamp Act crisis, 13, 15; attributed with *Disappointment*, 13,

40n.11; as author of *British Tyranny and American Chronicles*, 12–14, 40n.13, 92–93n.27, 108–9; commonplace book of, 13; family relationship with Franklins, Halls, Reads, 15, 29, 40n.18, 101n.31; marriages of, 14, 15; membership in Sons of Saint Tammany, 91n.17; as parodist, 30–37, 82n.5, 84n.19, 96–97n.33; on public vineyards, 15, 41n.23; on scholasticism, 103nn. 16 and 20; trades of, 14–15, 41nn.19 and 20. Works: *Fall of British Tyranny*, 13, 14, 15, 38, 40n.13, 41n.30, 91n.17, 92–93n.27, 108; *First of May, A New Song in Praise of St. Tammany*, 41n.30, 91n.17; *New Song, On the Repeal of the Stamp-Act*, 13, 15, 40n.10, 104n.4

Lee, Judge, 87n.50, 90n.6
Lee, Arthur, 92n.21
Lee, Gen. Charles, 108
Lee, William, 97n.2
Lemay, J. A. Leo, 40n.15, 41n.30, 86n.36, 87–88n.51, 93n.34
"Liberty Song," 92n.21
Liberty tree, 92n.25
Lilburne, John or Robert, 100n.30
Locke, John, 41n.30
Logan, James, 41n.22
London Chronicle, 83–84n.12
Louisburg, Battle of. *See* French and Indian War
Louis King of France (Louis XIV), 19, 104n.10
Ludlow, Edmund, 32, 47n.106

Macaulay, Catherine, 32, 47n.107, 93n.28
McCally, Hannah (Mrs. John Leacock), 14, 15
McCarter, Peter K., 96–97n.33
Macpherson, James, 103n.21
Magnus, Olaus (archbishop of Uppsala), 102n.14
Mandamus Council (1774), 27, 86n.41, 90n.6, 114
Mann, Horace, 28, 44n.76
Mansfield, William Murray, first Earl of, 19, 93n.28
Marston Moor, Battle of, 99nn. 20 and 27
Marvell, Andrew: *First Anniversary of the Government of O.C.*, 31-32, 46n.99

Massachusetts Charter of 1629, 18, 92n.24, 98n.7, 105n.18
Massachusetts Charter of 1691, 18, 98n.7, 105n.18
Massachusetts Gazette, 85n.29
Massachusetts Government Act (1774), 86n.41, 92n.26, 105n.18, 114. *See also* Coercive Acts
Massachusetts Spy, 24, 102n.8, 113–14
Mather, Cotton, 19, 43n.60, 96n.30; as Matherius Cottonius, 19, 96n.30
Matthews, Albert C., 29, 44n.76, 44–45n.82, 85n.29, 86n.35
May, Henry F., 47n.107
Mays, David, 40n.11
Mecom, Jane, 25, 84n.17
Mencken, H. L., 89n.71
Millenarian(s), 31, 37, 45nn.91 and 93
Millennial, 11, 12, 21, 30, 33, 36, 39, 45n.93, 47n.114
Millennialism, 11, 33, 34, 45n.91, 46nn. 97 and 100; civil, 25
Millennium, 11, 25, 33, 35, 43n.48; civil, 25
Miller, John C., 98n.7
Milton, John, 101n.31, 102n.14
Ministerial Catechise, 30, 45n.88
Monsieur de la Cutta de Bearda, 18, 102n.11
Montgomery, Robert, 108
Moore, Frank, 92n.21
Morris, Samuel, 14
Moses, Montrose J., 13, 40n.12
Mother Carey. *See* Carey, Mother or Sister
Mulford, Carla, 40n.10, 104n.4

Nelson, Thomas, 103n.22
New England Primer, 105–6n.25
New York Gazeteer, 98n.3
New York Journal or General Advertiser, 29, 30
Noble, Oliver: *Some Strictures upon the Book of Esther*, 30
Nonimportation, 16, 84n.23, 85nn. 28 and 30
Non-Importation Agreement (1765), 15
North, Frederick, 19, 30, 83–84n.12, 92n.26, 106n.28; as Haman the Northite, 19, 30, 83n.8, 99n.22
Norton, John, 103n.22

Obadiah, 26. *See also* Hancock, John

Occunneocogeecococacheecaheecadungo, 11, 17, 18, 91n.17
Ogilby, Martha (Mrs. John Leacock), 15
Old South Church, 85nn. 26 and 29
Oliver, Andrew, 83n.9, 83–84n.12, 87n.50
Oliver, Peter, 22–23, 43n.52
Oppenheim, Samuel, 45nn. 83 and 86
Ossian, 103n.21
Othniel, 27. See also Warren, John
Otis, James, 21, 92n.21

Paine, Robert Treat, 19, 20, 86n.39, 101n.6
Parable, biblical, 28, 29
Parliament, 32, 82n.2, 90–91n.12, 93n.28, 98n.7
Parody, 34–35, 37, 45n.90, 47nn. 118, 119, 120, and 121; parodic form(s), 11, 12, 17, 28, 36, 37, 45n.90. See also Satire, parodic
Patrides, C. A., 45n.91
Paterson, Stephen E., 42n.39, 43n.56, 44n.68, 83n.6, 85n.29, 90–91n.12, 92n.24, 94n.43, 99–100n.29
Paulding, James Kirke, 89n.71
Paxton, Charles, 83n.12
Peggy Stewart (ship), 19, 101n.2
Pennsylvania Chronicle, 91n.17
Pennsylvania Evening Post, 91n.17, 101n.31
Pennsylvania Gazette, 14, 15, 41n.24
Pennsylvania Packet, 48n.130
Philbrick, Norman, 13, 40nn. 14 and 16
Pitt, William, 13, 19, 104n.4; Pitites, 19, 104n.4
Platonists, Cambridge, 31
Political Register (London), 24
Pope Gregory Hildebrand (Pope Gregory VII), 19, 104n.12
Pope's Day, 36
Postmillennialism, 33
Powder scare, 26, 27, 86n.41, 87n.50, 88n.56, 89–90n.75, 90n.6, 94n.46, 114
Pownall, Thomas, 42n.35
Prescott, General, 108
Pride, Thomas, 100n.30
Privy Council, 16, 19, 82n.5, 83n.9, 84nn. 13 and 15, 92–93n.27, 105n.15; as Sanhedrin, 16
Prophecy, 11, 31

Provincial Congress, 90–91n.12, 92n.24, 99–100n.28, 101nn. 4, 6, and 32
Public Advertiser (London), 83n.8
Puritan(s), 25, 31, 32; anti-Catholic bias of, 18; Bible of, 81; complacency of, and jeremiad, 43nn. 60 and 62; millennialist vision of history of, and causes, 11, 34, 39n.1, 46nn. 97, 100, and 101, 97n.37; pamphlets of, 100n.30
Putnam, Israel, 11, 17, 18, 27, 35, 44n.74, 94n.46, 108; as Phineas, 17, 18, 27, 94n.46, 95n.14

Quebec Act (1774), 90–91n.12, 91n.16, 93n.28, 102n.11, 104nn. 4 and 9, 105n.21
Quincy, Josiah: Observations on the Boston Port Bill, 32

Rainsborough, Thomas and William, 100n.30
Read, Deborah (Mrs. Benjamin Franklin), 15, 45n.84
Read, James, 15, 29
Read, Joseph, 87n.50
Rees, James, 13, 40
Reformation, 30–31, 97n.37
Rehoboam, 90n.11. See also George III
Revenue Act (1764), 16
Revere, Paul, 90–91n.12
Reynolds, John, 100n.30
Rivington, James, 19, 98n.3
Rogers, John, 105–6n.25, 106n.26
Rogers, Nathaniel, 83–84n.12
Roman Catholic Church, 31, 45n.93, 98n.13, 103n.16, 106n.26. See also Catholics
Rose, Margaret A., 47n.118

Sabin, Joseph, 13, 40n.12
St. Peter's Church, 15
Sanhedrin, 82n.5. See also Privy Council
Satire, 12, 19, 24, 28, 34, 39–40n.8, 40n.17, 47n.117, 108, 109; parodic, 11, 12, 14, 17, 18, 20, 28, 29, 30, 34, 35, 37, 44n.76
Schlesinger, Arthur M., 12, 19, 39n.6, 41n.32, 92n.25
Scholasticism, 103nn.16 and 20, 108
Seabury, Samuel, 97n.1
Second Coming of Christ, 31, 33, 36, 45n.91, 46n.93

Seilhamer, George O., 13, 40n.12
Shipton, Clifford K., 20, 27, 42nn. 34, 38, 40, 41, 43, and 44; 43nn. 49, 56, 60, and 61; 44n.72
Simms, P. Marion, 81
Simon, 17, 18, 102n.9, 108–9
Sister Carey. *See* Carey, Mother or Sister
Skippon, Philip, 100n.30
Slotkin, Richard, 41n.30, 43n.60
Society for the Propagation of the Gospel in Foreign Parts, 105n.22
Society of the Sons of Saint Tammany, 15, 91n.17
Solemn League and Covenant, 23–24, 85nn.28 and 29
Song Now Much in Vogue in North America ("Liberty Song"), 92n.21
Sons of Liberty, Philadelphia, 15, 91n.17
Sprague, William, 21, 42nn. 35 and 43
Stamp Act (1765), 13, 16, 25, 29, 84–85n.23, 92–93n.27, 101n.4, 104n.4, 105n.21
Standing army, 25, 32, 47n.106
State in Schuylkill Fishing Company, 15
Stayner, Capt. Richard, 99n.16
Stein, Stephen J., 46n.97
Stewart, Anthony, 19, 101n.2
Stout, Harry, 46n.101
Stuart, Charles (King Charles I). *See* Charles I
Stuart, Charles (King Charles II). *See* Charles II
Stuart, John, third Earl of Bute. *See* Bute, John Stuart, third Earl of
Suffolk Convention, 90–91n.12
Suffolk Resolves, 90–91n.12

Tamanend, 15, 91n.17; as Tammany, 41n.30
Tea Act (1773), 16, 26, 82nn. 2 and 3, 105n.19
Teeter, Dwight L., 48n.131
Temple, John, 83–84n.12
Towne, Benjamin, 38–39, 48n.131, 101n.31

Townshend Acts, 16
Tuckerman, Frederick, 42n.35
Tyler, Moses Coit, 11, 12, 14, 19, 39n.2, 40n.9, 41n.32

Van Doren, 83nn. 8 and 9, 83–84n.12, 84nn. 13, 14, 16, and 17
Venables, Robert, 100n.30
Virga, Patricia H., 40n.11, 41n.22
Virginia (ship), 103n.22

Walpole, Horace, 28, 44n.76
Walpole, Sir Robert, 28
Warren, John, 27–28, 94n.47; as Othniel, 27, 94n.47
Warren, Joseph, 27–28, 85n.29, 86n.41, 94n.47, 108, 114; as "A True Patriot," 83n.10; as Caleb, 27, 88n.54, 94n.47
Washington, George, 98n.3, 108
Watson, John Fanning, 13, 40n.12
Wedderburn, Alexander, 16, 19, 83n.9, 84nn.13, 14, 16, and 17; as Wedderburnite, 16, 19, 84n.13
Wegelin, Oscar, 13, 40n.12
Wesley, John, 31
Whalley, Edward, 32
Whately, Thomas, 83–84n.12
Whately, William, 83–84n.12
Whately letters. *See* Hutchinson or Whately letters
Williams, Joseph, 19, 101n.2
Willoughby, Francis, 100n.30
Winsor, Justin, 96n.33
Wolfe, James, 19, 104n.9
Wood, Gordon S., 41n.25
Woodress, James, 44–45n.82

"Yankee," 93n.34
Yankee Doodle, 86n.36, 93n.34
Young, Alfred F., 32, 33, 39–40n.8, 46n.101, 47nn. 106, 110, 111, 112, and 117; 48n.125
Young, Dr. Thomas, 105n.19